Keeping Your Dividend Edge:
Strategies for Growing & Protecting Your Dividends

By Todd M. Wenning, CFA

Copyright and Disclaimer

For additional information, please contact Todd Wenning at http://www.toddwenning.com/contact.html

DISCLAIMER

Todd Wenning is a Research Analyst with Johnson Investment Counsel, Inc., an investment adviser registered with the U.S. Securities and Exchange Commission. The contents of this book express the opinions and views of the author alone and do not necessarily reflect the opinions or views of Johnson Investment Counsel or its employees. This book was prepared by Mr. Wenning in his individual capacity and not in his capacity as an employee of Johnson Investment Counsel. Johnson Investment Counsel disclaims responsibility for any private publication or statement of any employee.

The views and opinions presented in this book are intended for entertainment and educational purposes only and should not be construed as a solicitation to effect transactions in securities or the rendering of personalized investment advice. The views and opinions expressed in this book are not intended to be tailored financial advice and may not be suitable for your situation. No person should assume that any advice or strategies presented in this book serves as the receipt of, or a substitute for, personalized individual advice from an investment professional. You should consult with a professional where appropriate. The author makes no representations or warranties that any specific securities mentioned or investment strategies discussed are consistent with securities selected or investment strategies offered by Johnson Investment Counsel.

While the author has used best efforts in preparing this book, he makes no representations or warranties with respect to the accuracy or completeness of the contents of this book and specifically disclaims any implied warranties of merchantability or fitness for a particular purpose. The author shall not be liable for any loss of profit or any other commercial damages, including, but not limited to, special, incidental, consequential, or other damages.

The author or the author's employer may have positions or interests in the stocks mentioned in the book. These should not be viewed as recommendations; always do your own research before buying any stock.

To my lovely wife, Kate.

Contents

Introduction

He that can have patience can have what he will. –
Benjamin Franklin

At times it can seem like the deck is stacked against us as individual investors.

Institutional investors like mutual funds, endowments, and hedge funds have far more resources and tools than the weekend investor does. And we certainly can't out-trade the high-frequency trading programs.

What we'll always have on our side as individual investors, however, is our ability to be patient. It's a wonderful advantage not to be taken for granted. If our portfolios underperform a benchmark like the S&P 500 or the FTSE 100 in a given year, no one's going to pull money from our brokerage accounts. Instead, we're more able wait out intermittent storms to see the sun shine on the other end.

A gift often unused

Far too often, though, whether it's because we take it for granted or simply aren't aware of it, individual investors don't capitalize on this unfair advantage. Instead, we try to be like everyone else. We watch intra-day stock price changes, trade too frequently, buy high and sell low, and speculate on stocks in the news.[1] The result is usually poor returns. According to research by J.P. Morgan Asset Management, the average investor's return from 1995 to 2014 – a 20 year period – *was 2.5% annualized.* That's just 0.1% above inflation. Meanwhile, the S&P 500 returned 9.9% annualized and bonds returned 6.2% annualized.[2]

To improve upon these subpar returns, investors might consider extending their holding periods. Research conducted by The Motley Fool's Morgan Housel, for example, looked at U.S. market data stretching from 1871 to 2012, and found that the odds of you generating a positive return on an investment in the S&P 500 index increased from about 52% over a one day holding period (basically a coin flip) to 80% by five years and 100% by 20 years.[3]

While short-run results are largely influenced by chance and sentiment, over time, it's the business's fundamentals or broader market fundamentals that shine through. The market may not like a certain company today, this week, or next year, but as long as that company continues to generate profit growth over longer periods of time, it becomes much harder for investors to ignore it indefinitely.

Being patient sounds simple, but it's not easy. It's much easier to be patient when our stocks are marching higher. When our stocks are falling, however, we can end up doing stupid things and ultimately lose our edge over the market.

Enter dividends

What I've learned from other investors and from my own investments is that dividend-paying stocks can help you remain patient in the face of market turbulence and maintain discipline.

Here are a few reasons why:

• Dividends give us an alternative yardstick for measuring success. By turning our attention toward long-term income growth rather than near-term stock price fluctuations, we can remain focused on the economics of the business rather than fickle investor sentiment.

• Dividends need to come from cash produced by the company – they can't be faked or hid behind some accounting magic. As such, firms that pay dividends are more likely to generate consistent cash flows and can thus be considered higher quality relative to some of the more speculative and unprofitable firms often favored by individual investors.

• Dividend-paying stocks as a group are less volatile than non-dividend payers and tend to outperform non-dividend paying stocks during market downturns, particularly when dividends are reinvested.[4] This can help calm investor nerves when they might have otherwise sold in a panic.

Of course, the simple presence of a dividend paid by a company doesn't necessarily mean it will be a long-term winner, its management team isn't up to no good, or it won't be volatile in a down market. As we'll see throughout this book, however, companies with healthy and growing dividends can be an individual investor's best friend.

Changing dividend landscape

While the case for dividends remains robust, much has changed in the dividend world over the past 20 years. Consequently, investors should approach dividend investing with the following three points in mind.

First, more companies are using share repurchases, or buybacks, as an alternative to dividends for returning shareholder cash. Prior to the early 1980s, most companies used dividends to return the vast majority of their surplus cash to shareholders each year. Since then, however, U.S. (and increasingly non-U.S.) corporations have opted to use buybacks in lieu of making larger dividend payments. Because buybacks directly compete with dividends for a company's surplus cash, management teams (who often benefit themselves by using share repurchases) may opt to limit dividend growth in favor of buybacks.

Second, the financial crisis of 2008-09 witnessed the most dividend cuts since the Great Depression and had an impact on both corporate and investor expectations.[5] Indeed, some of the cuts made during the financial crisis came from companies that hadn't reduced their payouts in generations. After this carnage, investors can no longer simply assume that companies that have always increased their payouts will continue doing so.

Finally, the markets have become increasingly competitive with no signs of slowing anytime soon. According to the consulting group Innosight, the average lifespan of a company in the S&P 500 index fell from 61 years in 1958 to just 18 years in 2011.[6] Think about companies like Uber, which was founded in March 2009 and in a few short years completely disrupted the taxi and car-for-hire industry. As of this writing, Uber was valued at more than $50 billion.[7] **Facebook, Amazon, Netflix,** and **Google** – the so-called "FANG" stocks – all represent business models that couldn't have been fathomed in prior generations, yet they are among the largest businesses by market value in the U.S. today.

Dividend-paying large cap stocks in particular may be in the crosshairs of innovative companies, since these businesses often generate significant cash flows and have high profit margins that make them fat targets for upstart competitors. As Amazon founder and CEO Jeff Bezos once famously quipped, "Your profit margin is my opportunity," and he wasn't joking around.[8] Large, comfortable companies today must stay on the offensive or they might find themselves in the dustbin of dividend history. Just look at **Kodak** or **Nokia** – two former dividend-paying blue chips that fell behind on innovation and were unable to sustain their payouts.

This book addresses these three major changes and aims to help you navigate these tricky waters so that you can realize the edge that dividend investing has provided and can continue to provide for years to come. In the appendix, I've included a glossary of terms used in the book, a checklist for evaluating new dividend ideas, and a list of reading recommendations.

I hope you enjoy what follows. Your feedback – positive or negative – is appreciated and I can be reached via Twitter @toddwenning or through my website, www.toddwenning.com.

Chapter 1: Why Dividend Investing (Still) Works

"The prime purpose of a business corporation is to pay dividends to its owners. A successful company is one which can pay dividends regularly and presumably increase the rate as time goes on." – Security Analysis, Graham and Dodd

Ask most investors who has inspired their investment philosophy, and you'll likely hear legends like Warren Buffett, Benjamin Graham, and Peter Lynch mentioned. Though we have much to learn from these investors, the ability to fully mimic their success always seems disappointingly just out of reach for the everyday investor, who usually lacks the time, resources, and expertise that the investing "gurus" enjoy.

And this is *okay*. We have our advantages, they have theirs. The success stories of individual investors are far less well-known. It's their examples, however, that we can more credibly strive to mimic.

One of these unheralded investing legends is Anne Scheiber. After leaving work at the U.S. Internal Revenue Service in 1944, she invested $5,000 (about $68,000 in today's dollars) in blue chips of the day like **Coca-Cola** and Schering-Plough. At the time of her death in 1995 at age 101, she'd amassed a portfolio worth about $22 million – by my calculations, a 17.88% compounded annual growth rate – which was left as a donation to Yeshiva University.

A *New York Times* article profiling Ms. Scheiber had this to say about her investing approach:

In retirement, she embarked on her investment career with boundless vigor. Analyzing earnings reports, management philosophy and product quality, she bought into a variety of industrial companies and other blue chips...

Her investment strategies were simple, if not old-fashioned. Forget about market highs and lows on any given day, month or year. Reinvest your dividends. Hang tough and seldom sell.[9]

Those last three sentences are a brilliant summary of sound investing principles. They may sound "old-fashioned" in that they are not commonly adhered to by today's investors, but that makes them all the more valuable.

What I particularly like about Ms. Scheiber's story is that she didn't buy a bunch of shares and stuff the certificates in a coffee can for 51 years. She continued to monitor her investments while remaining patient. As we'll see in the coming chapters, this "watchful patience" mindset is critical in today's dividend environment.

And Ms. Scheiber isn't the only individual investor who made this approach work. Earlier in my career as a portfolio specialist (a fancy title for assistant) at SunTrust Asset Management in Washington, DC, I helped seven portfolio managers manage the accounts of some high-net worth individuals. What I learned from working with these individuals would forever change my investing philosophy.

A common thread shared by these successful individual investors was that they primarily owned dividend paying blue chips like **Procter & Gamble** and **3M**. These companies weren't

14

exactly obscure names back when they were bought, either - they were already among the largest companies in the U.S. market by the 1950s and 60s.

Remarkably, these investors hadn't taken flyers on faddish stocks of the day, but instead focused on blue chips with steady profitability and ample dividends. They kept tabs on the businesses and gave the investments time to flourish. Had they instead traded in and out of those same stocks every year, they would have inevitably racked up higher trading costs and taxes and likely bought and sold at inopportune times. Instead, these investors stayed patient and let the economics of the underlying businesses drive long-term returns.

Another thing that struck me was the tiny cost bases of some of their investments. A number of stocks in the portfolios had been held for 40-plus years, sometimes across generations, and bore cost bases that were a tiny fraction of the market price. More important than the cost bases, the fruits of their patience provided more than enough annual dividend income for them and their families without much need to touch the capital invested. For most individual investors, this is a dream retirement scenario.

Focusing on dividends

"Buying right and sitting tight" sounds simple, but it's definitely not easy to do over 30, 40, or even 50 years. The temptation to sell must have been strong at various times for these successful investors and I've often wondered how and why they held tightly onto their investments through volatile markets. I reckon a big part of it was due to the fact that many of them were business owners and understood that businesses shouldn't be judged in weeks and quarters, but in years and decades. Of course, the steady stream of dividend income these stocks generated each year didn't hurt, either. The dividends provided an alternative benchmark for measuring performance aside from the market price.

Here's what I mean. Consider a hypothetical 10 share purchase of 3M on January 2, 1970. This investment would have cost about $1,100 (about $6,800 in 2015 dollars). Your first quarterly dividend check would have been about $4.30.[10]

Five years later, your capital investment in 3M had actually lost a little money. Your quarterly dividend checks, on the other hand, increased to $6.80 - marking 58% growth. By this point, though, many investors would have bailed on 3M due to the lower stock price, even if 3M was outperforming the market on a relative basis.

Through January 4, 2016, assuming you didn't buy additional 3M shares, you'd have 160 shares (due to four 2-for-1 stock splits) worth over $23,000 – a 6.83% annualized capital return. In addition, your most recent quarterly dividend check would have been about $164 – nearly 40 times the amount of your first check, or 8.24% annualized.

Had you reinvested the dividends each quarter, your results would have been even better still. Assuming full reinvestment (no taxes or extra trading costs), your $1,100 initial investment would be worth approximately $63,856 and you'd have accumulated 435 shares that pay about $445 per quarter in dividends.[11] I imagine that someone who made this investment at 25-years old in 1970 would be pleased with either result now that he or she is in retirement and could start drawing on the dividend income.

This is admittedly a cherry-picked example and you could have just as easily bought and held a much worse-performing stock over the same period. That said, it does illustrate how, by focusing on the dividend growth rather than the fluctuating stock price, you can stay focused on long-term business fundamentals.

As U.K. fund manager Neil Woodford put it: "In the short-term, share prices are buffetted by all sorts of influences, but over longer-time periods fundamentals shine through. Dividend growth is the key determinant of long-term share price movements, the rest is sentiment."[12] Consider, for instance, 3M's long-term share price relative to its dividend per share growth.

Figure 1: 3M Share Price and Dividend per Share (trailing twelve month) History, 1970-2015

Source: Yahoo! Finance and author calculations, performance through December 1, 2015

As you can see, 3M's stock price ebbed and flowed over time as investor sentiment changed about the company and the market as a whole. The stock price ultimately followed the trajectory of the dividend growth. Why might this be? In the short-term, a stock may be out of favor due to various reasons, but in the longer-term, it's hard for investors ignore a stock that pays them increasing amounts of cash each year. Eventually, they sit up and take notice.

Dividend skeptics

Dividend-paying stocks fueled the returns of the investors I worked with and for many other individual investors I've met during my career. It's also worked over generations and across markets, as investment adviser Tweedy, Browne shows in its papers "The High Dividend Yield Return Advantage" and "What Has Worked in Investing".[13,14]

Despite this anecdotal and academic evidence, dividend investing isn't without its doubters. To defenders of the efficient market hypothesis and "rational" markets, for instance, dividend-focused strategies can seem irrational and an anomaly. Indeed, some behavioral economists chalk up dividend strategies to investor biases such as loss aversion, regret avoidance, and an inability to delay gratification.[15]

There may be grains of truth in each observance, of course, and it's important to consider alternative opinions, though I've yet to meet an investor employing any investment strategy who enjoys losses or embraces regret. Moreover, as we'll learn throughout this book, if there's any strategy that promotes patience over instant gratification, it's dividend investing.

The Oracle and Dividends

In his 2012 letter to shareholders, Warren Buffett made a compelling case as to why his company, Berkshire Hathaway, doesn't pay a dividend to its shareholders. Dividend skeptics often point to Buffett's comments as support for their argument. What the critics miss with Buffett's comments, however, is that Buffett was only referring to why *his company* doesn't pay dividends. Berkshire doesn't pay dividends, Buffett reasons, because he thinks he can manage the capital better than shareholders. And most would agree with him, including me.

Yet while he may not like *paying* dividends, Buffett certainly doesn't seem to mind *receiving* dividends. In fact, most of his largest holdings pay very ample dividends each year. Consider Berkshire Hathaway's top five holdings as of this writing:

Company	Dividend Yield (ttm)
Wells Fargo	2.71%
Kraft Heinz	3.16%
Coca Cola	3.02%
International Business Machines	3.72%
American Express	1.64%

Source: Company filings, Yahoo! Finance, as of January 2, 2016

One reason Buffett might like receiving dividends is it gives him cash to do what he does best – allocate capital. Yes, he could sell partial stakes of these businesses to raise cash, but the presence of a dividend also relieves him from making frequent buy or sell decisions.

Further, few management teams allocate capital as effectively as Buffett does. As such, most management teams should only have cash they need to reinvest in value-enhancing projects. All extra cash should be returned to shareholders.

As Benjamin Graham and David Dodd noted in *Security Analysis*, "A dollar is worth more to the stockholder if paid him in dividends than when carried to surplus [by the company]."[16] With few exceptions, I'd much rather have some of the firm's earnings in my pocket each year than leave it all in the company's coffers. Even well-run companies can succumb to internal and external pressures to do something on the M&A front and potentially destroy shareholder value. Having an appropriate dividend policy in place can help management focus on efficiently allocating its remaining capital. We'll discuss management's impact on dividends further in chapter five.

Considering buybacks

As mentioned in the introduction, corporate buybacks have surged in popularity as an alternative means of returning shareholder cash. Indeed, with the exception of 2009, in the U.S. market, gross buybacks have outpaced dividends paid each year since 1997.

Figure 2: Dividends and Gross Buybacks Paid in U.S. Market 1980-2014

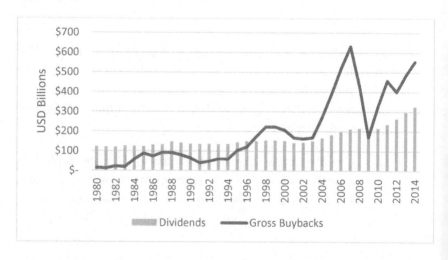

Source: Credit Suisse HOLT, Thomson Reuters DataStream, and author estimates

To see how this came about, we need to time travel back to 1982, when the U.S. Congress passed a new regulation (Rule 10b-18, to be exact) that gave corporations "safe harbor" to repurchase their own stock without liability for stock price manipulation, given certain conditions.[17]

It took the dotcom boom of the late 1990s for buybacks to really catch on. One of the major reasons for this was buybacks allowed companies, who were increasingly using stock options to pay and incentivize employees, to offset the share dilution that came with the option issuances.

From the company's perspective, there's really a lot to like about buybacks. In addition to offsetting stock option dilution, buybacks are more flexible than dividends (i.e. shareholders don't see them as an annual commitment), they can be used to manage earnings per share, adjust the firm's financial leverage, and provide a "signal" to the market that management thinks the stock is undervalued.

From the dividend investor's perspective, however, the benefits aren't quite as obvious. That said, buybacks are here to stay, so we might as well learn to tell the good ones from the bad.

Stock buybacks, when used appropriately, can be a dividend investor's ally if – and only if – the stock is undervalued when repurchased by the company and there are no better investment options (e.g. expand the business, acquire another company, etc.). It's really that simple. When the stock is undervalued, there's a wealth transfer from former shareholders to ongoing shareholders. This should be welcomed by dividend investors.

Buybacks can also help income investors by reducing the number of shares over which the company has to pay dividends. This in turn can drive dividend growth. For example, if a company with 1,000 shares outstanding pays $1,000 in dividends in year 1, it pays $1 per share ($1,000/1,000). If, in the following year, the company buys back 100 shares (10% of the total shares) and still pays $1,000 in dividends, its dividend per share is now $1.11 ($1,000/900).

Here's an example of a company that's properly using buybacks. U.K.-based retailer, **Next**, has a stellar track record of both buying back its stock and simultaneously increasing its dividend. In fact, from 2006 through 2015, Next reduced its share count by nearly 38%, or 5.1% annualized, in addition to growing its dividend 14.6% annualized.[18]

Figure 3: Next plc Dividend and Share Price History, July 2000–December 2015.

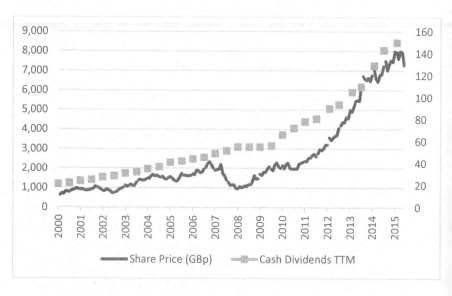

Source: Next plc, Yahoo! Finance, Author Estimates. Does not include special dividends. All figures in GBp.

What makes Next exceptional is that it's laid out clear rules for buying back stock, which it shared in its 2013 annual report.

1. *Share buybacks must be earnings enhancing and make a healthy Equivalent Rate of Return.*
2. *Only use the cash the business does not need. Next has always prioritised investment in the business over share buybacks.*
3. *Use surplus cash flow, not ever-increasing amounts of debt. We have never allowed our share buyback programme to threaten our investment grade credit status and will not do so going forward.*
4. *Maintain the dividend at a reasonable level through growing dividends in line with (earnings per share). Next will continue to increase dividends in line with EPS.*
5. *Be consistent. Next has been buying shares every year for more than 10 years, reducing the shares in issue by more than 50%.*
6. *For share buybacks to be an effective use of shareholder cash, the core business must have the prospect of long term growth.*[19]

The trouble is that most companies lack this sort of buyback discipline nor do they have a great track record of buying their stock at good prices. As the following chart shows, buybacks at the market level tend to ramp up when the market is high and trail off when the market is low. The exact opposite of what you'd like to see.

Figure 4: Gross Buybacks vs. SPDR S&P 500 ETF (SPY), 2004-2015

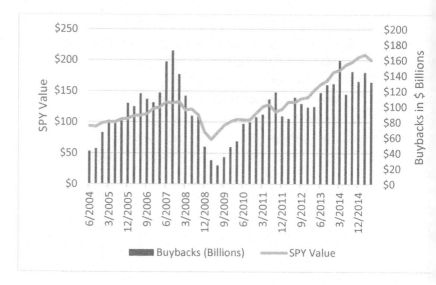

Source: Standard & Poor's, Yahoo! Finance, and author estimates.

Henry Singleton, the legendary CEO of **Teledyne**, adeptly repurchased his company's stock in the early 1970s - long before buybacks were popular - and put it this way: "If everyone is doing (buybacks), there must be something wrong with them."[20] As such, if you're researching a company with a track record of announcing massive buybacks when everyone else was doing the same thing, it's best to question management's buyback skill.

Some have reasonably argued that if you own and hold onto a company that's buying back its stock, you're implicitly agreeing that the stock is trading at a good-to-fair price. In turn, you shouldn't be upset if management buys back stock. If you think the stock is overvalued, you should sell it yourself. There's some truth to that. If you think the stock is *materially* overvalued (i.e. it's reaching what you consider irrationally high levels) you should indeed consider selling it. However, since income investors are primarily concerned with income growth and capital growth second, we're not interested in selling a stock just because it might be slightly overvalued. This action might not only trigger a capital gains tax, but we'd also need a better place to put the money. We'll discuss strategies for selling dividend stocks in chapter eight.

Shareholder yield

Because buybacks are here to stay and are an alternative for returning shareholder cash, some investors contend that the traditional "dividend yield" metric has less value compared to a "shareholder yield" metric that includes net buybacks (shares repurchased minus shares issued) and dividends. Though buybacks should indeed be considered as part of the return to shareholders, there are some theoretical problems with merging the two components.

First, as we discussed earlier, is that buybacks treat shareholders differently depending on whether or not the stock is underpriced, overpriced, or fairly-priced. A cash dividend always treats shareholders equally. Second, a company could repurchase a lot of its stock at an overvalued price, thus producing a deceptively high shareholder yield. Finally, the buyback component of shareholder yield isn't as reliable as the dividend component on a year to year basis. The company could simply cut back on share repurchases if it falls on tough times, producing a lower "buyback yield" while the dividend yield increases.

This isn't to say the buyback or shareholder yield has no merit, but I'm skeptical of lumping all buybacks in with dividends as they are two very different methods of returning shareholder cash. As such, income-minded investors should continue to rely

25

on dividend yield as the primary measure for cash return and valuation considerations.

Bottom line on buybacks

Dividend investors shouldn't dismiss buybacks altogether. While many companies misuse buybacks, when they're employed properly, they can help augment both your capital return and your income return. As you research dividend-paying companies that also use buybacks, ascertain whether or not the company has consistently repurchased stock in the past, what prices it paid, if it's buying back stock for the right reasons (i.e. valuation, not simply to offset dilution or artificially boost EPS), and if the buyback has a higher priority over the dividend.

Firms that are able to consistently generate enough cash to commit to a dividend and are confident enough to raise their payout each year are probably doing something right. A progressive dividend policy – i.e. one that aims to increase the payout each year alongside earnings growth - also shows a company's shareholders that it views them as partners in its prosperity.

Show me the money

You won't find this in any finance textbooks, but dividend investing works precisely because it encourages investors to think like investors – that is, thinking like a part-owner, buying good companies at good-to-fair prices, and holding them patiently.

- ➤ Dividend investing encourages investors to think like investors.
- ➤ Focusing on dividend growth rather than share price fluctuations can help you maintain a long-term approach.
- ➤ Buybacks are here to stay as an alternative to dividends, but most companies don't implement them appropriately. Companies with good buyback strategies, though, can be a dividend investor's best friend.
- ➤ Dividend investing is supported by both academic and real-world evidence.

Chapter 2: 10 Common Mistakes Made by Dividend Investors

> *It is remarkable how much long-term advantage people like us have gotten by trying to be consistently not stupid, instead of trying to be very intelligent. – Charlie Munger*

Over the years, I've compiled a list of common mistakes made by dividend investors – many of them also committed by yours truly at one time or another – that I hope will help you sidestep trouble down the road. As the above quote from Charlie Munger notes, you can increase your odds of success by simply avoiding dumb decisions rather than striving to outsmart everyone.

#1) Reaching for Yield

The first rule of dividend investing is that if a yield is too good to be true, then it probably is.

In the movie *Elf*, Santa gives Buddy the Elf some sage advice before he heads to New York City: "You see gum on the street, leave it there. It isn't free candy."

The same can be said for stocks with ultra-high dividend yields. There's almost always a catch. The market doesn't give away ultra-high yields (i.e. yields more than 2.5 times the market average) with little risk. If this were the case, investors would bid up the stock price so that the yield would conversely decline closer to the market average. Further, dividend yields rarely reach ultra-high levels due to dividend growth. Rather, ultra-high yields are almost always due to a depressed share price that typically accompanies poor business performance. Because of this, it shouldn't be surprising that dividend cuts frequently come from the top yield quintile.[21]

One of my first dividend investments was in a real estate investment trust called Education Realty Trust (today known as **EdR**), which owns and operates student housing around college campuses in the U.S. When I bought the stock in 2006, it was yielding about 8% and I recall thinking, "Even if the stock price doesn't go up, all I have to do is hold and I'll make 8% a year." By comparison, the S&P 500 was yielding about 1.7% at the time, so this seemed like a great deal, indeed.

Not long after I bought it, however, Education Realty Trust lowered its dividend payout as cash flows were pinched by higher-than-expected interest expenses and overhead costs, among other things. Fortunately, I exited the investment before things got much worse during the financial crisis.

I've spoken with a number of investors over the years who applied similar rationale behind buying an ultra-high dividend yield, I've yet to come across a story with a happy ending. Ultimately, my failed investment in Education Realty Trust amounted to a $160 loss – a small price to pay for such a valuable lesson that's saved me from making much more costly mistakes later on.

#2) Living in Low-Yield Land

In addition to buying stocks with ultra-high yields, dividend investors can make the opposite mistake by choosing stocks with yields that are too low. The justification for buying stocks with 1% to 2% yields in an income portfolio is often that they have stronger dividend growth prospects than those yielding 4% or 5%. From a strict income return perspective, however, it can take many years for a lower-yielding stock to match a higher-yielding stock's payout.

Consider the following scenarios:

- 5% yield; 4% annualized dividend growth
- 4% yield; 6% annualized dividend growth
- 3% yield; 7% annualized dividend growth
- 2% yield; 10% annualized dividend growth
- 1% yield; 15% annualized dividend growth

Figure 5: Hypothetical Dividend Growth Over a 10 Year Period

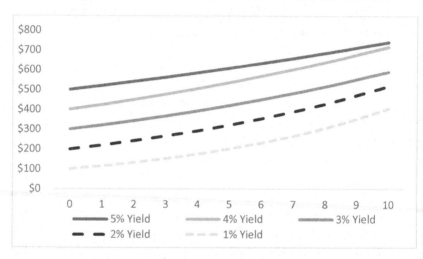

Ten years in, the 1% and 2% dividend yield examples are still producing far less income than the 3%, 4%, and 5% yield examples despite growing at double-digit rates.

"Ah," you might protest, "but shouldn't lower-yielding, higher dividend growth stocks have more capital return potential?" From a capital growth standpoint, what matters is the company's performance relative to investor expectations. In December 2005, for instance, **Wal-Mart** traded with a 1% dividend yield and grew its dividend at a 13% annualized rate over the subsequent ten years, but still underperformed the S&P 500 over that period by about 40 percentage points.

Conversely, tobacco company **Reynolds American** yielded over 4% in December 2005. Over the next ten years, Reynolds grew its dividend by 8% annualized and outperformed the S&P 500 by more than 200% over that period. What happened? Put simply, investor expectations for Wal-Mart in December 2005 were far higher than they were for Reynolds American. Even though both companies delivered solid results, Reynolds American beat expectations and the market awarded the company a higher price/earnings multiple, while Wal-Mart fell short of expectations and its price/earnings multiple contracted.[22]

So, if you don't want to shop the ultra-high yields or the ultra-low yields, where should you look for good dividend ideas? The "sweet spot" tends to be between 1-2 times the market average dividend yield. If the S&P 500 is yielding 2%, for example, my primary search would be between 2% and 4%. Anything lower than 2% isn't likely to produce enough income over the next 5-10 years and anything over 4% is pushing into higher risk territory. There are exceptions, of course, but the 1-2 times rule is a good place to start.

#3) Not Diversifying

It can be very tempting to load up on higher-yielding stocks to enjoy a larger amount of current income. As we discussed in the first mistake above, though, a high yield can also mean high risk to your dividend income stream if a few of your holdings cut their payouts. You may give up a little current yield by including some lower-yielding stocks with solid financials, durable competitive advantages, and a long growth runway in your dividend-focused portfolio, but what you lose in current income, you can make up for in income stability and growth potential.

Also, at any given time in the market, higher-yielding stocks tend to be concentrated in a few sectors. Utilities and telecommunications stocks, for example, traditionally have above-average yields. The trade-off is that they usually have lower relative earnings growth potential.

Disruptions in certain areas of the market can also increase yields in certain sectors. Leading up to the financial crisis, for example, bank stocks carried some of the highest yields in the U.S. market. A large investment in that sector may have produced significant amounts of income for a quarter or two but within a year many of the high-yielding bank stocks slashed their payouts.

In fact, in 2008, one of WisdomTree's ETFs - which was then called the "High-Yielding Equity Fund" (now called the WisdomTree High Dividend Fund (DHS)) – based its portfolio weighting by total dividends paid. Using this logic, a company paying out $500 in dividends would have a higher weight in the index than a company paying $250.

The approach apparently back-tested quite well, but by September 30, 2008, two weeks after Lehman Brothers filed for bankruptcy protection, more than half of the ETF's assets were in financial stocks.[23] At the time, its top holdings included **Bank of America**, which accounted for 10% of its net assets, **Citigroup** 7.5%, **JPMorgan Chase** 5.5%, **Wells Fargo** 5.2%, and **U.S. Bancorp** 3.2%. Within a few months each of these banks would cut its dividend, leaving investors in the strategy with a considerable income setback on top of a large loss in capital value.

I don't mean to pick on WisdomTree. I only use this example to illustrate the risks of not diversifying your dividend portfolio across sectors and focusing too heavily on high-yielding stocks. (To WisdomTree's credit, they've since capped the fund's single sector exposure at any time to 25% of net assets.)

This doesn't mean you should pick one or two high yielders from every sector just to call yourself diversified, either. You should still understand how each of the businesses work, what their risks are, and what role they play in your strategy.

#4) Not Paying Attention

Some dividend investors make the mistake of thinking that their work is done once they've bought a stock. Just sit back and watch the dividends roll in, right? When in doubt, erring on the side of patience is generally a good strategy, but beware of using patience as a cover for having to make a tough decision. There's a fine line between patience and laziness.

By no means should you spend your days watching your stock prices fluctuate, but do read through your companies' quarterly and annual reports to make sure each is still doing what you thought it was doing when you bought it.

In some cases, you'll find that you no longer recognize the business you originally bought or that the business is headed in a direction that you don't like. When this happens, you should consider selling and reinvesting the proceeds in a better idea. We'll discuss selling strategies in chapter eight.

#5) Ignoring the Balance Sheet

Equity owners are below creditors on the totem pole since the latter have contractual agreements with the company to have their money returned with interest. I's important to make sure that creditors are being taken care of before we can even think about dividends. In fact, creditors often attach covenants to their loans to ensure that the company will pay them back in full. If the company breaks those covenants (the details of which can be found in annual filings), the creditors may have the right to restrict dividend payments to equity owners.

Beyond the debts stated in a company's balance sheet, you should also look for "off balance sheet" items like underfunded pension exposure, legal settlements, and non-cancellable operating leases. If the company's pension is significantly underfunded (i.e. it has far more liabilities than assets), for example, the company will likely need to shovel cash into the plan each year to keep it solvent. This is cash that may have otherwise been returned as dividends. Such obligations could remain a millstone around the company's neck for many years and weigh down its ability to pay dividends.

#6) Not Remaining Calm & Balanced

The individual investor's greatest advantage is his or her ability to be patient, so it's important to use this advantage to the full extent. Remaining calm in the face of a 24/7 financial news cycle is easier said than done, of course, and a bad period in the market or for one of your stocks can produce undue stress. It's worth noting that investing-related stress can also come when things are going well just as easily as when they're not. What to do when your investment is up 50%, 100%, or more can itself be a difficult decision to make. Both enthusiasm and despair can both impact our decision-making processes.

As Credit Suisse's Michael Mauboussin has noted in various articles, when we're stressed, our mental time horizon shrinks and we have a tendency to make decisions that are completely focused on short-term results and we disregard long-term effects.[24] This reaction comes in handy when we're in actual physical danger, but it's the exact opposite of what we should do in investing. In Mauboussin's book, *More Than You Know*, he suggests that "The prescription (for dealing with stress in money management) is to work hard on maintaining an appropriate long-term focus."

How might we work to maintain an appropriate long-term focus? It helps to remember that the true benefits from dividend investing are realized only with adequate time. Further, we have much better odds of determining whether or not the underlying business is on the right path than guessing where the stock might trade in the next few months.

As such, your time is much better spent on getting to the bottom of the business issues than speculate on stock price behavior. If you've calmly and rationally evaluated circumstances and believe your thesis has changed, by all means take action, but don't get discouraged or encouraged by short-term market reactions.

#7) Relying Too Much on History

Over the last decade or so, a number of indexes have been created to identify companies with long track records of growing dividends – the best known are S&P's "Aristocrats" and NASDAQ's "Achievers." Though these lists are helpful for idea generation and they often include some well-run businesses, a dividend growth track record is no guarantee of future dividend growth. Good investing is not achieved while looking at the rear-view mirror. What matters is what lies ahead.

Yes, a company that's paid a growing dividend for 20 years or more may be a good *indication* that the company takes its dividend policy seriously, but a lot can change at a company over time. A new management team with a fresh growth mandate from the board, changing shareholder interests, or a series of bad acquisitions that leaves the company with a burdensome amount of debt can all lead a company to reevaluate its dividend policy.

It's important to consider a dividend track record in a broader context by asking questions like:

- How has the company's dividend policy changed over time?
- Has the company's competitive position improved or deteriorated over time?
- Is the company buying back more stock than it used to?

Not answering questions like these can create problems down the road. Taking a page from my own list of mistakes. Before its dividend cut in 2009, **Pfizer** had one of the best dividend track records in the U.S. market, having raised its payout for over 40 consecutive years. Before slashing its dividend in 2014, British grocer, **Tesco**, was long a staple in U.K. dividend portfolios and had raised its payout for more than 20 consecutive years. In short, I put too much faith in both companies' dividend history. Remember that when pushed to the financial edge, in the board's mind, history and tradition typically take a backseat to making sure the company can remain a going concern, maintain good standing with creditors, and otherwise create long-term shareholder value.

#8) Disregarding valuation

Consider two investors each of whom invested $100,000 in dividend portfolios with 5% starting yields. Over the course of ten years, each investor realizes annual dividend growth of 3%. The first investor (bottom line) bought stocks that were considerably overvalued and subsequently lost 20% in capital value in year one; alternatively, the other investor (top line) invested in stocks that were undervalued and gained 20% in capital value in year one.

After the year one corrections to fair value, both portfolios grew at 8% per year over the subsequent nine years.

Figure 6: Hypothetical Investments Over 10 Year Period

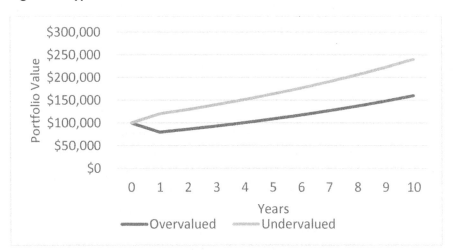

At the end of ten years, both portfolios generated the same amount of dividend income ($57,319), but their ending capital values are nearly $80,000 apart ($159,920 vs. $239,881). It's hard to imagine that the two investors would feel equally good about their performance even though they realized the same dividend income over the ten year period.

Here's another way to think about this difference. If both investors liquidated their dividend portfolios in year ten and invested their capital in bonds with 5% coupons, the first investor would receive annual interest payments of $7,996 while the second investor would receive $11,994 per year until maturity.

Though it's a hypothetical example, it illustrates an important point about the hidden costs of not paying attention to valuation in income investing. Ultimately, capital growth matters.

Whether you use relative valuation methods (i.e. comparing P/E ratios, etc.) or absolute valuation methods (i.e. dividend discount models, discounted cash flow models, etc.),

37

the important thing is to fully consider the price you're paying and the value you're getting from each investment. Get to know the businesses you'd like to invest in, understand what drives their performance, and don't rely on a single metric (e.g. dividend yield, price/earnings) alone to guide your buying decisions.

#9) Not using tax-advantaged vehicles

Dividend critics make a valid point that regular cash dividends create frequent taxable events while other methods of capital allocation (e.g. company reinvestment, M&A, buybacks) allow the investor to defer taxes until they sell some or all of their investment. While we can counter this argument by saying that the cost of companies retaining all of the capital and potentially misspending it can far exceed the taxes incurred by the dividend, we can't deny that there is, in fact, a tax on dividends that can be a drag on your long-term compounding growth potential.

To minimize tax drag, it's important to practice smart asset "location." To the extent possible, consider placing your higher-yielding stocks in tax-advantaged accounts (like IRAs in the U.S.) and your lower-yielding and non-dividend paying stocks in fully-taxable accounts.

#10) Equating bonds and dividend stocks

Dividend-paying stocks have a number of advantages and disadvantages over fixed-income product. One advantage is that they can battle inflation via rising payouts. As Peter Lynch wrote in *Beating the Street*:

> *Whereas companies routinely reward their shareholders with higher dividends, no company in the history of finance, going back as far as the Medicis, has rewarded its bondholders by raising the interest rate on a bond.*

38

That said, all stocks, whether they pay dividends or not, have a very different risk profile than bonds. Bonds can serve a critical purpose in many portfolios – particularly for those in retirement or living on fixed incomes – since their principal and interest are contractually agreed upon. Unless there's a major Enron-like blowup at the company and you're buying investment-grade bonds, you can feel confident that you'll get your principal back when the bond matures and collect interest along the way. If you buy U.S. Treasuries, you are *guaranteed* by the full faith and credit of the U.S. government to get your money back plus interest.

Stocks, on the other hand, don't have maturities or contractual obligations to pay you a dime. Shareholders are also further down the food chain from bondholders when it comes to bankruptcy settlements. The trade-off, of course, is higher growth potential from equities. As such, it's important to remember that a dividend stock is still a stock and it's not to be used as a swap for a bond when you primarily desire capital preservation.

Key Takeaways

- ➢ The difference between strong and middling returns often comes down to how many pitfalls you've avoided. By knowing what to avoid ahead of time, you can save yourself from making these critical mistakes.
- ➢ Don't get greedy - a dividend yield that seems too good to be true probably is.
- ➢ Approach buying, holding, and selling decisions from a position of patience.
- ➢ Think like a business owner and never buy a dividend-paying stock without understanding how the company makes money.

Chapter 3: Evaluating Dividend Ideas

"The principle difficulty in your case," remarked Holmes in his didactic fashion, "lay in the fact of there being too much evidence. What was vital was overlaid and hidden by what was irrelevant. Of all the facts which were presented to us we had to pick just those which we deemed to be essential, and then piece them together in their order, so as to reconstruct this very remarkable chain of events." - Arthur Conan Doyle, *Sherlock Holmes, The Adventure of the Naval Treaty*

When it comes to equity analysis, a lot of attention is paid to valuation. And rightly so, as your investing career will likely be a short one if you consistently overpay for assets. Even among income-minded investors, though, surprisingly little attention paid to dividend-specific analysis. That is, analysis that concentrates on the company's ability to sustain and grow its payout over time.

Despite the plethora of data at our fingertips today, what dividend research there is tends to begin and end with earnings-based dividend cover. As long as the company is earning more than it's paying out, the thinking goes, all is well with the dividend. Conversely, if the company is paying out about the same amount as (or more than) it's earning, the dividend is at risk.

While earnings coverage is important, in my experience, the main causes of a dividend cut are factors *other* than a low dividend cover (or a high payout ratio). Indeed, low dividend cover today is usually symptom of larger problems that have existed for some time.

Rather than just looking at the earnings-based dividend cover, it seems prudent to take a more holistic approach to dividend analysis. Here are the factors I find to be most useful in measuring a company's ability to sustain and grow its payout.

- **Sales growth**: Sales are the life-blood of a company. If sales are drying up, that puts added pressure on profits and cash flows and thus the dividend, too. It could also be a signal that the company is currently in or is approaching liquidation phase. In other words, the company is deliberately shrinking the business by selling assets to pay out cash to shareholders. Because of this, you want to see companies with three-year sales growth of at least 3% annualized.

- **Interest coverage (operating profit/interest expense)**: If a company is struggling to pay the interest on its debt, its creditors and the credit ratings agencies will take notice. This will likely lead to credit rating downgrades and a higher cost of borrowing for the company. Consequently, this could pressure net income and cash flows and thus the dividend. In a worst-case scenario, the dividend could be cut to accelerate the repayment of principal. Look for consistent interest coverage of at least 2.5 times for larger cap non-financial stocks and 4 times for smaller non-financial stocks. These levels are a decent proxy for investment-grade credit ratings.[25] Even if the company has an official credit rating from S&P or Moody's, checking the interest coverage is a good cross-check.

- **Net debt/EBITDA (earnings before interest, taxes, depreciation & amortization)**: This is a common measure ((Debt − Cash) / EBITDA) that creditors and

41

ratings agencies use to determine credit quality and it's often used as a metric in debt covenants. A firm that has borrowed too much or is struggling to pay down its debt relative to its profitability is more likely to have a risky dividend. An appropriate net debt/EBITDA ratio will vary by industry (e.g. regulated utilities can usually bear higher ratios), but anything above 4 times is usually a sign that the company has too much debt. In general, look for companies with net debt/EBITDA ratios below 2 times.

• **Dividend growth rate**: A slowing dividend growth rate could be a sign that the business is also slowing down. Eventually, all companies' dividend growth rates decline, but you want to see a steady decrease over many years and not a sharp drop. All other factors held equal, a three-year annualized dividend growth rate of at least 7% is generally a sign that management and the board are confident in the business's medium- to longer-term prospects.

• **Earnings cover**: Even though I don't think it's the best measure of dividend health, earnings cover (net income/dividends paid or earnings per share/dividends per share) remains the most common metric cited by both companies and investors alike, so it should be considered in any dividend analysis. A steady earnings cover of at least 1.5 times (67% payout ratio) is a good cutoff for measuring dividend sustainability and growth potential. In most cases you'll want to see at least 2 times coverage (50% payout ratio), particularly if the company still has decent growth opportunities.

• **Free cash flow cover**: Free cash flow cover ((Cash from Operations − Capital Expenditures) / Dividends Paid) is a better measure of dividend health than earnings cover because companies don't pay out earnings – which are an accountant's opinion – they pay out cash. As such, I'd rather look at a company's cash flows than net income as a way to measure dividend sustainability and growth potential.

Free cash flow cover can be thought of as your dividend "margin of safety" or "margin of error." All else equal, the higher the ratio, the more secure you can consider the current payout and the more likely the dividend can grow in the future. Conversely, a firm with a free cash flow payout ratio near or below 1 times has very little margin for error. If the firm falls on a rough year, the dividend might be on the chopping block.

A company with low or non-existent free cash flow cover could support the payout for a short time using alternative financing (borrowing, selling assets, cash on hand, etc.), but that's an unsustainable solution. Eventually, the firm needs to generate free cash flow from operations to support the dividend.

Here, I would also look for consistent 1.5 times free cash flow coverage (67% payout ratio) to feel confident in the dividend's sustainability and growth potential. Companies with more stable demand, like a large tobacco company, may be able to comfortably maintain a lower free cash flow coverage ratio since their cash flows are more predictable and there's less growth opportunity. These are more the exception than the rule.

• **Operating margin**: A company with diminishing operating margins (operating profit / sales) could be facing increased competitive pressures or becoming less efficient. When this occurs, less money falls to the bottom line and to cash flows. Consequently, the dividend can become riskier.

As a rule, I look for companies that are consistently generating operating margins above 10%. There are some exceptions. A few sectors like grocery and retail, which we'll see in a moment, carry low-single digit margins and make up their returns by rapidly turning over their inventory. Cyclical companies' margins will also naturally ebb and flow. In those cases, use rolling 5-year average margins to account for the company's profitability over a business cycle.

• **Return on equity**: Companies that are able to consistently generate returns on equity above their cost of equity – and do so with appropriate amounts of debt – are probably doing something right. A good rule of thumb is to screen for companies that consistently generate at least 10% returns on equity. If you prefer to use return on invested capital instead of return on equity, I would also use 10% as my baseline figure for identifying promising companies.

{You may notice that these criteria don't fit well with financial stocks (e.g. banks, insurers) and real estate investment trusts (REITS). I've provided additional criteria for evaluating them in the appendix.}

Putting it all together

If you use these metrics in a stock screener, you'll likely find that very few companies pass the test. The companies that do pass the test are worth further research, of course, but that doesn't mean the dividend-payers that don't pass should be dismissed, either. The above criteria should mainly be used to evaluate new and existing holdings to determine where the company may have strengths or weaknesses. For example, a company that passes the return on equity threshold but has poor balance sheet metrics may be highly-levered and should therefore be approached with caution.

Similarly, a slow-growing stock that carries a 5% dividend yield and is growing its payout around 5% a year may be a very fine investment, even though it doesn't pass the 7% dividend growth threshold. Still, the criteria require you to recognize that the low dividend growth rate is likely an indicator that the company is late in its mature growth phase and to be on the lookout for signs of diminishing prospects.

In my experience, the most reliable red flag has been a lack of free cash flow cover. If a company checks off all the other boxes but fails on free cash flow, it tells me I need to do some more digging. Is the company selling assets or borrowing to maintain the dividend? Does the company's line of work necessitate a high level of capital expenditures? Getting answers to these questions will help you get a more complete understanding of the company's business and its ability to fund and grow its payout.

Pay particular attention to the company's metrics over time and take note of any trends. As we'll see in the coming chapters, companies with declining free cash flow or deteriorating balance sheets can be early signs of trouble ahead.

Finally, you can use these criteria for evaluating opportunistic purchases. If a particular stock falls on hard times and its dividend yield becomes more attractive, as long as it passes most of the above tests, it could be worth further research. In this situation, if I'm initially unfamiliar with the business, I'll also incorporate some broker forecasts for revenue, earnings, and free cash flow to see if I might be missing something important in the company's near future. Though broker forecasts can be unreliable at times, if brokers and sell-side analysts are predicting a sharp drop in revenue or earnings in the next two years, you'll want to find out why that's the case, since it could mean weakening dividend health in the near future. While these metrics shouldn't be used as a definite buy or sell signal, they can help you separate potentially attractive situations from those best left alone.

Eschew obfuscation, espouse elucidation

Even if a company passes all of the above criteria and its dividend looks healthy, if you don't understand how all the parts of the business work, it's best to walk away. Now, some investors like to dig into complex business models because they can present overlooked opportunities that others have tossed into the "too hard" pile. However, opaque business models can also be fertile ground for management mistakes or plain fraudulent behavior.

After an hour of research, if it isn't clear how the business makes its money, there's a good chance that either the company intended for that to be the case or the people at the company don't understand it themselves. Both scenarios are less than ideal for making a long-term investment and you'll save yourself a lot of trouble by avoiding them. Instead, dividend investors should prefer to own companies with understandable business models and those that provide their investors with plenty of data for evaluating their progress.

Einstein reportedly remarked that if you can't explain a concept to a six-year-old child, you don't understand it yourself. That's a pretty good benchmark for evaluating business models, as well. **Wells Fargo**, for example, focuses on traditional banking (i.e. attracting deposits and making loans) and has a far simpler business model than **Bank of America**, which, in addition to traditional banking has large investment bank and trading operations. Between these two banks, then, I would start my research with Wells Fargo since I think I can better explain in simplistic terms how the bank makes its money.

This doesn't mean that an attractive company can't have multiple divisions or operate in more than one industry, but it should be clear how each of those segments make money, what each of their strengths and weaknesses might be, and how they fit into the company's long-term strategy. Dividend investors should pay particular attention to the business segments that account for more than a third of the company's overall operating earnings (EBIT) since they will have a considerable impact on profits and free cash flow (business segment information can be found in a company's annual filings).

Key takeaways

- ➤ In addition to considering valuation, income investors should spend time assessing whether or not the dividend is sustainable and able to grow in the coming years.
- ➤ Watch for trends in the metrics over time. As we'll see later in the book, deteriorating fundamentals and usually a good sign that the dividend is in trouble.
- ➤ It's a good rule to walk away from dividend-paying stocks with complex business models. If you can't see explain how a company makes money and how it funds its dividend, it's hard to be confident in the company as a long-term investment.

Chapter 4: Durable Advantages & Dividends

"The successful investor is usually an individual who is inherently interested in business problems." - Philip Fisher[26]

One of my favorite TV shows is *Shark Tank* (if you're outside the U.S. you may be more familiar with *Dragon's Den*) – a program where nervous entrepreneurs pitch their business ideas to five venture capitalists in the hope of getting equity investments. One of the things I like about the show is the quality of the questions asked by the investors ("The Sharks") to the entrepreneurs. Some typical questions include:

- What prevents another company from doing what you're doing?
- Do you have any patents?
- How much does it cost you to make a unit? What do you sell the product for?
- Is this your first time as an entrepreneur or have you started other companies before?
- How much of your own money have you invested in the business?

These are all questions that investors (as opposed to speculators) should ask before making an investment. These business-focused questions seek to understand the quality and growth potential of the business and the owner's motivations.

While there are differences between venture capital investments and public market investments, both represent ownership stakes in the underlying business. Participants in the public markets, however, often lose sight of this connection between the stock and the ownership stake it represents.

Investors often mistakenly buy a dividend-paying stock based solely on metrics like dividend yield, price/earnings ratio, or on tips they've read about or heard from a friend. They don't take the necessary time to get to know the business in which they're taking an ownership stake. Given the competitive intensity in today's market, a long-term investment made without consideration of the company's competitive position is pure folly.

A recent paper by Martin Reeves, Simon Levin, and Daichi Ueda in the *Harvard Business Review* studied the longevity of 30,000 U.S. companies over a 50 year period and found that corporate lifecycles are shrinking faster today than in prior decades.[27] In fact, they show, "Public companies have a *one in three chance of being delisted in the next five years*, whether because of bankruptcy, liquidation, M&A, or other causes. That's six times the delisting rate of companies 40 years ago." (My emphasis added.)

Here's a particularly important point for dividend investors to consider: the study found that "the rise in mortality applies regardless of size, age, or sector."[28] In other words, buying a large cap stock and thinking that makes you safer from competitive threats could be a costly mistake indeed. Larger companies have their benefits, to be sure, but they can also fail to be adequately nimble in rapidly-changing markets due to the bureaucracies and legacy issues (e.g. the "we've always done it this way" attitude) that often occur in businesses with thousands of employees.

Start digging

So, how can we begin to find companies able to fend off these fierce competitive threats? It's easier to determine which companies have durable advantages with hindsight, but as investors we must consider what a company's advantages might be over the next five to ten years and beyond. In my experience, the best way to get started is to put on the right hat – the business analyst's hat – when you research a company.

In the 1987 Berkshire Hathaway annual report, Warren Buffett relayed to the company's shareholders that, "When investing, we view ourselves as business analysts - not as market analysts, not as macroeconomic analysts, and not even as security analysts."[29] You can spot the difference between a business analyst's way of thinking and a market, macroeconomic, and security analyst's way of thinking by the questions they ask.

A market analyst, for example, might ask how the stock could perform in an early stage or late stage of a bull market, a macroeconomic analyst how the stock could fare in a certain interest rate environment, and a security analyst how the company's price/earnings ratio compares with its peers. These are all fair questions to consider, but they don't address some fundamental factors a long-term investor should consider.

A business analyst, on the other hand, will ask questions like those asked by the Sharks at the start of this chapter: Who are the major competitors? Why is capitalism letting this company earn great returns on its investments? What are management's capital allocation priorities? These are questions an intelligent investor should ask before taking an equity stake in any company – whether it's the successful dry cleaner down the street or the largest company in the S&P 500.

One of the principal objectives of business analysis is understanding the company's competitive position and whether or not it will be able to maintain its success for a decade or more to come. This ability to think long-term is another unheralded advantage for individual investors. Fewer investors than you might imagine are thinking 3-5 years out, let alone ten or more.

Consider this passage from a *Wired* interview with Amazon founder, Jeff Bezos:

> *If everything you do needs to work on a three-year time horizon, then you're competing against a lot of people. But if you're willing to invest on a seven-year time horizon, you're now competing against a fraction of those people, because very few companies are willing to do that.*[30]

The same can be said for investing in the public markets, which are crowded with individuals and entities concerned with short-term performance, whether by choice or compulsion.

For dividend investors, we specifically want to know if the company can maintain and grow its cash flows over the long term. This requires a vision into the company's prospects well beyond the average investor's time horizon, which in turn requires a serious consideration of how the company will protect its profitability in a very uncertain future. When companies' competitive positions erode, there will be increased pressure on cash flows and therefore the dividend itself, so we're compelled to give a company's competitive dynamics some thought – both before and after we make the investment.

Protect the castle

Years ago, Warren Buffett coined the phrase "economic moat" to describe businesses with durable competitive advantages. These advantages enable companies to consistently protect their economic "castles" from the relentless forces of capitalism, sustainably generate returns above their costs of capital (i.e. create shareholder value), and reliably produce cash flows across the market cycle.

It's important to separate companies with true durable advantages and those with only temporary advantages. From time to time, companies can catch a trend or phase and produce tremendous results for a year or two. Eventually, competition steps in or trends change and the company returns to generating middling returns. All else equal, these are businesses we want to avoid buying – at least at a rich price.

There are various ways that a company can realize durable competitive advantages. **Coca-Cola**, for instance, derives some of its durable advantages from its globally-recognized brand. Importantly, Coca-Cola's brand has allowed it to consistently charge a premium price compared to competitors that are essentially selling the same sugary-water mix.

Still, it would take decades if not generations (and a whole lot of luck) in order for another soda maker to approach the global recognition and consumer preferences that Coca-Cola currently enjoys. Coca-Cola's brand advantage (as well as its massive distribution network), enabled the company to consistently generate high returns on invested capital and produce generous cash flows that also helped fuel annual dividend growth for over 50 years.[31]

Figure 7: Coca-Cola Monthly Share Price vs. Dividends per Share (ttm), 1962-2015

Source: Yahoo! Finance, Author Calculations. Split-adjusted share prices used. Dividends per share plotted on right axis.

Moat evaluation

Determining whether or not a company truly has a sustainable competitive advantage or economic moat is more art than science. Even the best business analysts can get it wrong from time to time, but it doesn't mean we shouldn't try.

Here's why. Dividend investors are primarily concerned with whether or not a company's dividend is both sustainable and able to grow over the long-term. Without the potential for steady profitability over the course of a number of business cycles – implying an economic moat is present – those essential ingredients are compromised. A company that is able to regularly raise prices on its products without losing a large chunk of customers or manufacture products at a cost well below those of its competitors, will, all else equal, have a healthier dividend.

To get started, here are some questions to ask yourself as you evaluate new ideas or current holdings in your portfolio for a potential economic moat.

Pricing power

Does the company have a recognizable brand? If so, does the brand enable the company to charge higher prices for its products?

A brand without pricing power does not an economic moat make. Most consumers have heard of **General Motors**, for example, but few would be willing to pay a dollar more for a GM car than a similar car made by **Ford** or another mass-market competitor. A car made by **Ferrari**, on the other hand, is a different story. Consumers *are* will to pay a premium price to own a Ferrari, in part because of the luxurious, timeless image and the "status" that comes with driving one of those cars. A quick look at these companies' gross margins illustrates the stark differences in pricing power.

	2013	2014	TTM
Ferrari	47.1%	45.5%	48.3%
Ford	12.8%	12.4%	14.3%
General Motors	11.6%	8.9%	11.7%

Source: Morningstar.com, as of January 4, 2016.

Are competitors unable to enter the company's market?

Government-issued patents allow the inventor of a product to realize monopoly rights to the product for a certain period of time, typically for 10-20 years.[32] Assuming it's a product that consumers want, a patent can be extremely valuable as it can give the holder a decade or more to realize high returns on their investment. Medical device company, **Medtronic**, for example, has raised its dividend for 38 consecutive years. It has been able to do so, at least in part, because it has a portfolio of valuable patents that's allowed it to charge high prices and consistently produce significant cash flows.[33]

Government-issued licenses and regulations can also prevent new competitors to enter a company's market. This is evident in the waste management business, for example, where the regulatory costs, permits, and citizen opposition to new landfills allow incumbents to generally enjoy high profitability.

Beware, however, of firms that rely too heavily on a single patent, license, or regulation to drive their profitability because if and when the patent or regulation expires, the business may have to change dramatically and the dividend may be at risk.

Are there considerable costs for customers to switch to a competing product?

Think about a product that you use regularly either at home or at work. This could be a software program, a subscription service, or a special type of equipment that you've been trained to work on and is an integral part of your daily routine. Now think about how much it would cost you in either time or money to change to another product. If the costs are burdensome, the company selling you that product may have a durable switching cost advantage and it can probably charge you higher prices each year.

An example of the switching cost advantage can be found in **Jack Henry & Associates**: a Monett, Missouri-based provider of computer systems and software solutions to small banks and credit unions. Jack Henry provides mission-critical products to banks where the cost of failure is quite high. Because Jack Henry has a great reputation for being a reliable provider of these services and employees at thousands of banks around the country have been trained on its software, its customers aren't likely to quickly change providers. Indeed, Jack Henry's customer retention rate has been consistently over 95% and over the last fifteen years ended September 2015, its dividend growth rate has exceeded 15% annualized.[34,35]

Does the company have high recurring revenue?

Companies that generate more than half of their annual revenue from recurring sources (i.e. membership sales, consumables, etc.) not only help dividend investors rest a little easier since they can be more confident in future sales coming in, but this can also be indicative of a switching cost advantage. About 90% of **Ecolab**'s revenues, for example, are recurring in nature. This high level of recurring revenue can be attributed to its razor-and-blade business model through which Ecolab leases cleaning equipment to customers that can only use its proprietary chemicals.[36] This favorable business model has helped drive 24 consecutive years of dividend growth.[37]

Does the company have a location advantage relative to its peers?

This advantage largely pertains to materials and commodity companies who have access to scarce natural resources or have lower transportation costs to major demand centers. One example is **Compass Minerals**, which operates large rock salt mines in Ontario, Canada and Louisiana that have excellent water transportation access via the Great Lakes and the Mississippi River, respectively.

Compass Minerals' location advantage matters because salt has a low value-to-weight ratio, making transportation costs an important component of total cost. This allows Compass Minerals to deliver salt to municipalities for deicing roads at the same price as competitors, but at a lower cost, leaving more profit on the table for Compass.

Does the company have strong employee relations or a good corporate culture?

The cost of frequently training new employees is not only a negative on the income statement, but the company also loses valuable institutional memory with the departure of each good employee. One of the many reasons that **Costco Wholesale** has stood apart from other retailers is that its employee turnover (6% in 2014) is far below the retail industry average. This keeps long-term costs down even though Costco pays its hourly employees above-average wages, with health benefits in most cases.[38]

Costco co-founder and former CEO Jim Sinegal once noted that "Culture isn't the most important thing. It's the only thing," and much of Costco's success can be linked to its vibrant culture.[39] Despite the importance of corporate culture, I have never come across a sell-side research report that discusses corporate culture in any depth. We're doing ourselves a disservice by ignoring it. That's because, when an energetic and authentic culture complements a company's durable competitive advantages, it can yield great results for shareholders.

To some, culture may seem like nice-but-ultimately-inconsequential items, but as Buffett pointed out in his 2005 letter to Berkshire shareholders, the little things that companies do each day matter over time:

> *If we are delighting customers, eliminating unnecessary costs and improving our products and services, we gain strength...On a daily basis, the effects of our actions are imperceptible; cumulatively, though, their consequences are enormous.*
>
> *When our long-term competitive position improves as a result of these almost unnoticeable actions, we describe the phenomenon as "widening the moat."*[40]

Culture matters precisely because it allows for these small actions to occur and can thus have a tremendous impact on a company's competitive position. As long-term, business-focused investors, it's well worth our time to consider culture as part of our regular research process and how it may contribute to - or, in cases of a poor culture, even detract from - the company's ability to create shareholder value for years to come.

One way to learn a company's culture is to read through its Glassdoor reviews to get a general sense of how employees view the company. Also read through the company's career page on its corporate website. Does it have good benefits? How many people is it hiring today and for what positions? Is this a company that you'd like to work for? If the company regularly lands a spot on a national or local "Best Places to Work" list, it could also be a sign that its employees are happy and productive.

Does the company have a unique manufacturing, distribution, or production process that enables it to realize per unit costs well below those of its competitors?

One question I always ask companies is, "If I had $1 billion of capital, what stops me from entering your industry and cutting into your profits?" The reason I ask this is if the opportunity is there, capital will find its way into the industry, even if it costs a billion dollars to get started. There has to be *something* about the business or the industry, beyond the amount of money needed to get started, that keeps competitors and their capital at bay.

UPS and **FedEx**, for example, have established such wide-reaching distribution and logistics networks that a would-be competitor would not only need untold billions to gain a foothold in the U.S. domestic shipping market, but they'd also need strong demand for their services to cover the high fixed costs that come with the territory. UPS and FedEx, in contrast, have already established networks that enable them to deliver goods at a much lower per unit cost than anyone else. Germany-based competitor, **DHL**, tried to unseat UPS and FedEx's U.S. dominance in the mid-2000s, but ultimately lost $10 billion over five years and shut its U.S. domestic express delivery in 2008.[41] While FedEx doesn't pay a robust dividend, UPS has more than quadrupled its dividend since 2000 and typically carried a 2-3% dividend yield since 2006.

Not a panacea

Correctly identifying dividend-paying companies with economic moats derived from either pricing power or cost advantages (ideally both!) can lead to very satisfactory returns if they are purchased at good-to-fair prices. However, as Buffett has suggested, economic moats are either widening or narrowing at all times.[42] A competitive position is never permanent in capitalism, and it has never been truer than today. Because of this reality, dividend investors should be vigilant about the trajectory of their companies' advantages over time. A rapidly shrinking moat can lead to rapidly deteriorating profit margins and cash flows and therefore pressure the dividend.

How might you be able to sniff out a shrinking moat before other investors? Two things I look for are intensifying mergers and acquisitions activity and rapidly slowing dividend growth rates. On M&A, if a company hasn't historically made acquisitions a priority and suddenly feels the need to aggressively acquire other companies, it might be losing faith in the growth potential of its core operations. This new strategy could due to new market entrants, softer pricing, or some other competitive threat.

Similarly, if a company's annual dividend growth rate suddenly slows from, say 10%, to 2% and doesn't operate in a highly-cyclical industry, it could be a sign that the board of directors is less confident in the company's ability to afford its payout over the next 3-5 years. Beyond this, if you can find evidence of price erosion, cost overruns, or formidable new market entrants, it's time to reconsider your investment thesis.

Key takeaways

> Because of globalization and rapid technology advances, companies today are likely operating in the most competitive period in history. As such, we would do well to consider a company's competitive position before making a long-term investment.

➤ Before making the investment, make sure you're able to explain how the company can protect its profitability over the next ten years or more. Does it come from brand, switching costs, lower production costs?

➤ Companies with deteriorating competitive advantages may be under more pressure to slow dividend growth, halt the dividend, or cut it altogether.

Chapter 5: Management Matters

"Stated simply, two companies with identical operating results and different approaches to allocating capital will derive two very different long-term outcomes for shareholders." – William Thorndike, *The Outsiders*

Over the years, I've been fortunate to be invited to speak about finance and investing at a number of elementary and junior high schools. Without fail, I'm asked after every presentation if you need to be good at math to be an investor. I reply that you can't be afraid of numbers, but most of the math I do is basic arithmetic with a little algebra here and there.

This often comes as a surprise to the students – and the adults in the audience – because many of them think investing is all about math. As such, for those who aren't confident about their math skills, investing can seem very intimidating. It doesn't have to be that way.

Certainly, the financial markets are a math-oriented person's dream. There are always numbers to crunch and different ways to analyze the data. Naturally, then, investing attracts a lot of quantitatively-skilled people who love putting their skills to work. Because of this dynamic, a few myths about investing have emerged:

- People who are good with numbers think they'll be great at investing,
- People who *aren't* good with numbers think they'll be bad at investing, and
- People think quantitatively-heavy analysis is superior to qualitative analysis.

None of these commonly-held beliefs are necessarily true. I may be biased since I'm not a quantitatively-minded person myself, but my experience has taught me that while a basic understanding of math and accounting is essential for investors to know, it's the *qualitative* analysis that sets investors apart.

Anyone can crunch numbers on an Excel spreadsheet and most investors do. It's far rarer to see investors considering the intangibles like competitive dynamics, corporate culture, and management skill. It's in these qualitative factors where truly differentiated and insightful research can be created.

We've already addressed competitive dynamics and culture, so let's have a look at management analysis.

Management's impact on dividends

When times are good at a company, an otherwise poor management team can be made to look more skillful than they actually are. As such, we want to look beyond recent outcomes and instead focus on management's capital allocation *process*. In his book, *The Success Equation: Untangling Skill and Luck in Business, Sports, and Investing*, Michael Mauboussin observes that:

> When a measure of luck is involved, a good process will have a good outcome but only <u>over time</u>.[43] (Mauboussin's emphasis)

As dividend investors, we want to identify – ahead of time - the management teams that have prudently established the right dividend policies, conservatively finance their operations, and skillfully allocate capital in a way that benefits long-term shareholders. Management analysis not easy and it's not foolproof, but making the effort is worthwhile as it can also help us identify value-destructive management teams. Knowing which management teams to avoid can be just as valuable as knowing which ones are worthy of our backing.

Ultimately, management teams can do four things with their cash flows:

1. Build up cash/pay down debt
2. Spend it on acquisitions
3. Reinvest it in the business
4. Distribute it to shareholders (dividends and buybacks)

How management allocates capital between these options can have a tremendous impact on the long-term value of the business. These decisions can quickly turn an otherwise good business into a middling one within a decade. Consider Buffett's observation in the 1987 Berkshire Hathaway shareholder letter:

> *The lack of skill that many CEOs have at capital allocation is no small matter: After ten years on the job, a CEO whose company annually retains earnings equal to 10% of net worth will have been responsible for the deployment of more than 60% of all the capital at work in the business.*[44]

Dividend cuts often follow a string of poor capital allocation decisions – i.e. management made aggressive and expensive acquisitions, over-levered the balance sheet, didn't innovate enough, etc. As such, as dividend investors, we'd be remiss to overlook the importance of management.

The right-sized sandbox

When researching management's relationship to the dividend, one of the best things you can do is determine if the company's dividend policy provides management with the right-sized "sandbox" in which to allocate capital. What I mean by this is, does management have too much capital at its disposal, too little capital, or does it have the right amount?

Ideally, management teams will retain only the cash they need to reinvest in value-enhancing projects and return the rest to shareholders. More commonly, they retain too much cash and end up feeling it burning a hole in their pocket. This is typically when you see management hubris rear its ugly head – "transformative" acquisitions are made, cavalier buybacks are executed, corporate jets are purchased, and so on.

In fact, a 2003 study by Robert Arnott and Clifford Asness found that, contrary to the popular assumption that low dividend payout ratios translate into higher earnings growth, the opposite is more the case.[45] Why might companies with high dividend payout ratios drive stronger earnings growth? One reason suggested by Arnott and Asness is that because these companies have less cash left over after the dividend is paid, they're less likely to engage in value-destructive empire building. Further, with a limited budget, the management teams need to be more selective with the projects they choose.

On the other hand, when you buy shares of a company that doesn't pay a regular dividend, you're putting total faith in the management team's ability to allocate capital on your behalf. Frankly, there are very few companies that deserve this level of trust, either because the managers aren't skillful capital allocators or they have more cash than they need. Put simply, most companies shouldn't have a full-sized sandbox.

Here's the other extreme. U.K.-based insurer, **Admiral Group**, pays out all surplus cash to shareholders each year. Since becoming public, Admiral's paid a "normal" dividend and a "special" dividend amounting to all the cash that's left over the company's met regulatory capital needs and maintained the business.

It's a different approach, for sure. In a 2010 interview with *The Telegraph*, Admiral's founder and outgoing CEO Henry Engelhardt's explained the reasoning behind the unique dividend policy:

65

"We believe in thrift. We believe that money hurts companies...One of the reasons we pay the dividends we do is that if we left the money in the company, we'd probably waste it."[46]

I've yet to come across another company with that particular approach. While I'm sure there are times when Admiral's shareholders would have benefitted from the company retaining and reinvesting some of that cash, I find this approach refreshing. How many CEOs would so readily admit that they'd probably waste surplus cash?

Most companies fall somewhere in between a full sandbox and an empty one. What we want to avoid are situations where the sandbox is too big and management is destroying shareholder value or conversely the sandbox is too small and management is desperate for capital to grow the business.

Digging into the details

Analyzing management teams can admittedly be challenging for individual investors. Compared with professional investors, we typically lack direct access to the C-suite or to sell-side analysts who themselves have regular access to management. Despite this obstacle, thanks to public filings, earnings call transcripts, and Google searches, you can find out quite a bit about management from the comfort of your home office.

Before buying any dividend-paying stock, I recommend seeking answers to the following questions:

Does the company have the right dividend policy?

A company's dividend policy should be considerate of the business's cyclicality, capital intensity, and its reinvestment opportunities. It should also be clear, consistent, and affordable.

Commodity-based companies like miners and oil & gas producers, for example, tend to be both cyclical and capital intensive in nature. Management teams and the boards of such companies tend to get in trouble by raising their dividends too quickly when commodity prices are high and they're flush with cash. When commodity prices fall and they need capital, though, they often end up cutting the payout. This does not entice a patient, long-term shareholder base.

Rather than pursue an aggressive and progressive dividend policy, leadership teams of commodity producers should either target a small percentage of net income as their "normal" dividend and pay an additional "special" dividend in particularly good years, or tie their dividend payout to the underlying commodity price.

Both strategies acknowledge the cyclical and highly uncertain nature of their operations and make it clear to shareholders that the dividend will fluctuate over time. Indeed, a special dividend policy can serve as a pressure-release valve of sorts since it can relieve management of a cyclical company of the problem of having too much cash near the peak of their business cycle.

Though the company's share price has languished in the face of declining gold prices in recent years, I respect **Eldorado Gold**'s dividend policy, which is directly linked to the price of gold and production.

> *We have a simple, sustainable dividend formula based on the average realized gold price and the number of ounces of gold sold. It's a tiered approach, so as the average realized gold price increases, the fixed dollar dividend amount also increases.*[47]

Eldorado Gold may not be an anchor in a dividend-focused portfolio, but at least as a prospective shareholder you have a clear understanding that the dividend policy isn't a traditional progressive one. It's clear from the start that you'll likely have fluctuating payouts year by year.

If a cyclical company doesn't employ one of these preferable policies, you can check dividend affordability by calculating normalized earnings per share and dividing it by the current dividend per share. You can calculate normalized EPS by taking the average of the last five to seven years' return on equity (an approximate business cycle) and multiplying that figure by the latest book value per share.

To illustrate, if a company's ROEs over the past five years were 10%, 0%, 15%, 6%, and 30% (average 12.2%) and the current book value per share is $10, you could estimate normalized EPS as $1.22 (12.2% x $10). If the current dividend is $1 per share, caution is warranted. One bad year and the dividend could be at risk. If the dividend is $0.60 per share, however, you're in better shape, assuming there hasn't been a material change in the business, as the company is covering its payout more than twice over with normalized earnings.

On the other end of the spectrum, management teams at more defensive businesses like telecoms, tobacco companies, and utilities should, all else equal, pay out a higher percentage of earnings and free cash flow as dividends. Cash flows at such companies are often more predictable, their industries typically feature high barriers to entry, and reinvestment opportunities are usually limited.

Whatever the nature of the underlying business, I prefer to invest in companies with clear dividend policies (i.e. "We target a free cash flow payout ratio of 40%) rather than one that simply says the dividend "is at the discretion of the board of directors," or some variant thereof. Companies in the former camp are more likely to consider the dividend as an ingrained part of their culture and have seriously considered their capacity for paying the dividend. The latter, by not defining their dividend policy, indicate either a lack of thoughtfulness about the dividend, a non-committal attitude, or a highly-uncertain operation. None of these are signs that long-term dividend investors want to see.

What are management's capital allocation priorities?

A company's capital allocation priorities change from time to time to adjust to market opportunities. Sometimes buybacks are more attractive, sometimes M&A targets are more plentiful, or perhaps management wants to quickly pay down debt it took on to make an acquisition. Changes can also occur when a new management team comes on, particularly if a new CEO has a growth mandate from the board after years of sluggish performance. Management strategy changes are normal and can be healthy, but dividend investors should be mindful of where management places the dividend on the priority list over time.

One way to do this is to read the company's last five annual reports, flip through some investor presentations (usually found on the company's investor relations website), and the last five full-year earnings conference call transcripts. What you should be looking for are references to the dividend. Has management's language changed (i.e. has it switched from an enthusiastic tone to one that's more cautious) or has it been consistent?

Moreover, while reading the last five years' worth of filings, you also want to determine if management has delivered on its strategy over time. If not, what changed and why?

Does the company have the right amount of leverage?

Similar to the previous discussion about the right dividend policy, a company's borrowings should be reflective of the cyclicality and capital intensity of its operations. A highly cyclical company should, all else equal, maintain much lower leverage ratios (e.g. debt/EBITDA, gearing, etc.) than a company in a defensive industry like consumer staples, utilities, and telecom.

Leverage cuts both ways and while a highly-levered commodity producer can generate outsized returns for shareholders when commodity prices are surging, a massive loan taken near the top of the cycle can make the subsequent down-cycle much more painful for shareholders. The company may be forced to sell valuable assets, put important long-term investments on hold, or cut its dividend to remain solvent.

In fact, as we'll discuss in chapter six, one of the major reasons that companies decide to reduce their payout to shareholders is a desire to remain in good standing with the credit markets. Because of this, it's best to be cautious with companies that rely too heavily on debt. Be sure to compare the company's credit ratios to its peers and watch for developing trends over time.

Is management properly incentivized to support the dividend?

How management is paid and incentivized is detailed either in the proxy statement (in the U.S.) or in the board of directors' remuneration report found in the annual report. This is a critical but often overlooked discussion that can help you understand what motivates the management team and how they will think about capital allocation.

Be sure to understand on which metrics the board has decided to base management's annual and long-term incentives, and how those incentives might impact the dividend. Ideally, you want to see a good balance between metrics that support dividend sustainability (earnings, free cash flow) and smart growth (return on equity, return on capital, etc.).

Remarkably, a recent study by IRRCi found that 75% of companies in the S&P 1500 don't use any balance sheet/capital efficiency metrics like ROIC, ROE, or Economic Value Added (EVA) in determining long-term management incentives.[48] This opens the door to management pursuing growth-for-growth's-sake and can increase the odds of management destroying shareholder value. In turn, this increases the risk for a dividend cut.

Key takeaways

> Management analysis is more qualitative in nature, but it doesn't mean that it's not important.
> If you invest in a company that doesn't pay a dividend, you're making an outsized bet in management's capital allocation skill; however, highly-skilled capital allocators are a rare breed.
> Higher dividend payout ratios can actually lead to stronger earnings growth.
> Read through the past five years' worth of a company's annual report and always ask, "How might this impact the dividend?"

Chapter 6: Avoiding Dividend Cuts

An ounce of prevention is worth a pound of cure. –
Benjamin Franklin

Dividend cuts have a devastating impact on income investors, particularly those who are harvesting dividends to supplement their retirement incomes. Not only is your income slashed, but the stock price has probably declined markedly, making it far more difficult to reallocate your capital to another investment and produce similar levels of income.

Even for investors with longer time horizons, dividend cuts can be a material setback. A dividend that's been cut in half, for example, and subsequently grows at an 8% annualized rate (which may be an optimistic pace in some situations) would take about nine years to get back to pre-cut levels. Even with a multi-decade time horizon, nine years is a good amount of time.

In recent years, much attention has been paid to the increasing number of companies raising their dividends, which has indeed been impressive. What's been less discussed, however, is that the number of U.S. companies cutting or suspending their dividends has also been increasing. In 2015, this increase was primarily driven by companies whose profits depend on commodity and energy prices.

Figure 8: Number of U.S. Companies Lowering or Omitting Dividends, 2004-Present

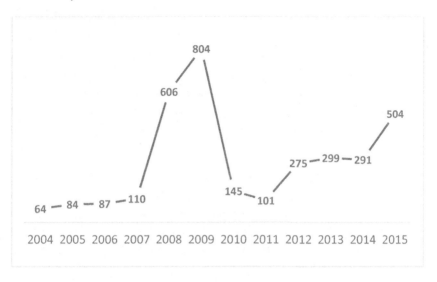

Source: S&P Dow Jones Indicies; As of December 31, 2015; Author Calculations[49]

With the frequency of dividend cuts and omissions on the rise, it's important to understand why companies cut their dividends in the first place and how we might avoid them with our current and future investments. In this chapter, we'll discuss three case studies that I think represent the most common reasons for dividend cuts.

No Such Thing as a Safe Dividend

Case Study: Exelon

Utilities are often mistakenly considered to be "bond alternatives," meaning investors sometimes view a utility stock's dividends as near-certainties not so different risk-wise from interest payments received from bonds. Though you should never confuse bonds with equities (dividend-paying or not), decades ago, utilities were mainly regulated monopolies that controlled the energy production process from start to finish for a certain region. This allowed them to generate steady and very predictable profits each year, which helped secure dividend payments.

This dynamic has changed considerably in recent decades as deregulated activities have taken a larger share of many utilities' operations. While deregulation opened the possibility of higher earnings growth rates for some utilities, it came at the expense of earnings predictability and thus the security of the dividend.

In October 2000, for example, Chicago-based electric utility **Exelon** was formed through a merger between PECO Energy and Unicom. Over the next eight years, Exelon broadly outperformed its peer group as measured by the **Utilities Select Sector SPDR ETF** and more than doubled its dividend between 2001 and 2008.

This success was fueled by growth in its un-regulated business that relied heavily on wholesale natural gas prices remaining elevated in the U.S. market. Natural gas prices plunged during the financial crisis, however, and never fully recovered due in part to rapidly increasing domestic natural gas production. Exelon's growth strategy consequently stalled. In February 2013, Exelon cut its dividend by more than 40%.[50]

**Figure 9: Exelon Monthly Price vs. Dividend per Share (ttm),
November 2001 – December 2015**

*Source: Yahoo! Finance, Author calculations. Share price
is split-adjusted. Dividends per share (right axis)*

Could we have seen the dividend cut coming? By 2011,
Exelon wasn't covering its dividend with free cash flow and the
dividend was held flat for two years. In 2012, interest coverage
(EBIT/interest expense) plunged, putting the company's credit
rating at risk. By themselves, any one of those factors was a red
flag, but together they spelled disaster for the dividend and the
writing was (with the benefit of hindsight) on the wall well before
the dividend cut.

	2012	2011	2010	2009	2008
Free cash flow coverage	0.20	0.58	1.38	2.04	2.57
Earnings coverage	0.68	1.79	1.85	1.94	2.05
Dividend per share	$2.10	$2.10	$2.10	$2.10	$2.03
Interest coverage (EBIT/interest expense)	2.64	6.39	5.97	7.26	7.58

Source: Company filings, author calculations

Lessons learned: Exelon

- **Commodity prices cut both ways:** Anytime you invest in a dividend-paying stock whose profits heavily depend on a prevailing commodity price – whether it be energy, agriculture, metals, etc. – it's important to consider how prepared the company's financials are for a downswing in the major commodity price. As we discussed earlier, companies in capital intensive industries and those with cyclical business models should, all else equal, have conservative dividend policies. Because Exelon became more of a cyclical business, it should have adjusted its dividend policy accordingly, paying out a lower percentage of profits and cash flow or adopt a flexible dividend policy.

- **Careful with companies walking the junk rating line:** In its February 2013 press release explaining the rationale for the reduced dividend, Exelon noted that the cut would help the company maintain its investment-grade credit rating.[51] Companies that need steady access to the debt markets are loathe to see their credit ratings fall below investment-grade status into "junk" status as it can mean a significant jump in borrowing costs and thus lower profitability.

A major reason for this typically sharp increase in borrowing costs from investment-grade to junk status is that many institutional funds, insurance companies, and banks are restricted to owning just investment-grade debt. As such, if you own a company that uses a lot of debt and has credit ratings near that investment-grade/junk line (e.g. "BBB-" for S&P or "Baa3" for Moody's), the dividend may be in danger if the company runs into short-term trouble.

• **Lack of free cash flow cover is unsustainable:** If companies are unable to fully cover their dividends with free cash flow, they need to fund the payouts with cash on hand, debt, or asset sales. None of these arrangements are sustainable in the long-run. Firms in the materials or energy sectors can at times get walloped by a sharp decline in commodity prices and need to temporarily fund their payouts with alternative sources. Eventually, however, companies need to generate more than enough free cash flow from ongoing operations if they are to maintain the dividend.

Institutional Imperative

Case Study: Pfizer

In July 2008, just as the financial crisis was picking up steam, I bought some shares of the pharmaceutical giant, **Pfizer**. At the time, Pfizer had a trailing dividend yield of 6.9%. I thought this was a slam dunk investment. After all, Pfizer had increased its dividend for over 40 consecutive years, had recently boosted its payout by 10%, had a *AAA-rated* balance sheet, and was in a defensive industry that should, it seemed, hold up relatively well in a poor economy.[52] Even with Pfizer facing generic competition and slowing sales, declining dividend coverage, and a well-above average dividend yield, it seemed Pfizer was well-positioned to withstand some short term turbulence.

	2008	2007	2006	2005
Revenue (million)	$48,296	$48,418	$48,371	$51,298
Dividends per Share	$1.28	$1.16	$0.96	$0.76
Free cash flow cover	2.04	1.41	0.80	1.56
Earnings cover	0.94	1.01	2.77	1.43

Source: Company filings, Author calculations.

A few months later in January 2009, I was having lunch with a colleague and we began discussing the sweeping dividend cuts that were occurring at the time. "I'm shocked at the types of companies that are cutting their payouts," I remember him saying, "**General Electric, Dow Chemical**...and today was Pfizer."

I nearly spit out the water I'd just sipped. *Pfizer?!* My friend must have been mistaken. Alas, he was not.

While announcing a massive $68 billion acquisition of fellow drug giant, Wyeth, Pfizer's board said it was cutting its once-sacred dividend in half.[53] The capital markets were tight during the financial crisis, but Pfizer, backed by its near-perfect credit rating, nevertheless raised the debt it needed to help fund the stock and cash deal. Clearly it wasn't a funding issue.

So, why the need for the dividend cut? The answer might be found in the press release for the acquisition, which mentioned the dividend remained "competitive with other industry participants."[54] In other words, Pfizer's board wasn't happy that its yield was much higher than its peers – for most of 2008, Pfizer's yield ranged between 1-2 percentage points above most of its competitors. I think the board saw the acquisition and the numerous dividend cuts occurring elsewhere at the time as an opportunity to reduce its payout.

Figure 10: Pfizer Monthly Price vs. Dividend per Share (ttm), January 2005 – December 2015

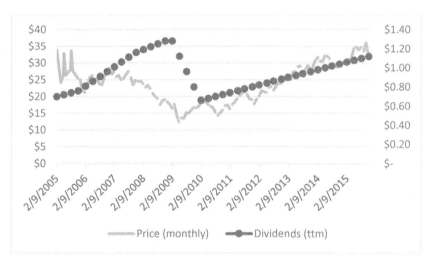

Source: Yahoo! Finance, Author calculations. Dividend per share (right axis)

As of this writing six years later, Pfizer's dividend has yet to fully recover from its pre-cut levels.

Lessons learned: Pfizer

- **Beware of "transformation" stories:** Going back as far as Pfizer's 2005 annual report, the company often spoke of the need to transform the business in the face of patent expirations, the need for cost reductions, and replenishing the drug pipeline.[55] In 2008, restructuring costs were on the rise, reaching $2.68 billion (5.5% of sales) that year, up from $1.3 billion spent in each of the previous two years.[56] My rule of thumb is that a company gets one year to transform itself – if the transformation stretches into multiple years, the company is likely struggling to gain traction in its new strategy. A dividend cut could be on the table.

• **Be mindful of competitors' dividends:** Companies' boards don't operate in vacuums and most monitor their competitors' dividend policies as a guidepost for their own. Buffett calls this the "institutional imperative" and noted in the Berkshire Hathaway 1989 annual report that "the behavior of peer companies, whether they are expanding, acquiring, setting executive compensation or whatever, will be mindlessly imitated (by institutions)."[57] If a company's dividend yield is well above its peer group average or if peers are cutting their dividends, the board may be more inclined to follow suit.

• **Don't depend on dividend track record:** Prior to the dividend cut, Pfizer had one of the most dependable dividend track records in the S&P 500. Yet when it came down to it and the board changed its strategy, the dividend was unceremoniously slashed. A long history of increasing dividends is a positive signal, of course, but shouldn't be a major factor when there are other red flags present.

• **Shrinking sales have rippling effects:** Revenues are a company's lifeblood and are at the top of a company's income statement for good reason. If customers aren't coming through the door, it doesn't matter how efficiently you can produce the item or how progressive your dividend policy is. As such, when companies see demand falling for their products and they're unable to offset it with price increases, they're forced to reduce costs in order to maintain and grow profits and cash flows. If a company is unable or unwilling to reduce expenses or doesn't see a recovery in demand in the near future, the board may be more inclined to reset investor expectations around the dividend. Sluggish sales could also lead the board to pursue a more aggressive M&A strategy to reignite growth, which could also result in a reevaluation of the dividend policy.

Bad Investment Decisions

Case Study: Tesco

Britain's largest grocery chain, **Tesco**, was long considered a core holding of U.K.-based dividend investors (and was once one of mine, as well). In fiscal year 2011 (year-end February 2011), for example, Tesco increased its dividend by 10.8% - marking an impressive 27 consecutive years of dividend increases.[58] At the time, well-respected long-term investors like Neil Woodford and Warren Buffett held considerable positions in Tesco, suggesting the company passed their well-regarded filters. In addition, Tesco's UK market share was over 30% and its domestic dominance appeared safe. All seemed to be right.

A prong of my initial thesis on Tesco were that the company's mis-timed expansion in the U.S. (Fresh & Easy) would eventually stabilize and rebound as the U.S. economy recovered – particularly in the Western U.S. states where the stores were located. Further, I thought Tesco's investments in China would fuel earnings and dividend growth for years to come. Finally, I believed the U.K. market would continue to produce plenty of cash flow to support international growth.

81

Then the wheels started to fall off one at a time.

My U.S. turnaround thesis fell flat. In April 2013, Tesco announced it was exiting the U.S. market and Fresh & Easy filed for bankruptcy protection. All of this resulted in over a billion dollars in trading losses and impairments.[59] That in itself should have been a sign to sell.

I rationalized, however, that with the Fresh & Easy chapter finally shut, Tesco could better focus on its other global operations. Strike one.

Tesco also never figured out how to turn a steady profit in China. Ultimately, Tesco entered into a joint venture with a large Chinese retailer who actually knew how to run a retail business in China. So much for the region fueling dividend growth. Strike two.

With Tesco's focus on its struggling international operations, it began losing ground to competitors in its home market. Indeed, a space race and pricing war simultaneously erupted between Tesco and other U.K. grocers like **Sainsbury's** and **Morrisons**. Meanwhile, discounters and higher-end, specialized grocers alike feasted on the opposite ends of the pricing spectrum.

Even though Tesco seemed best suited to survive this war of attrition, profit margins suffered. This put further strain on both free cash flow- and earnings-based dividend cover. In response, Tesco held its dividend flat starting with the interim dividend paid in December 2012 and in February 2014 abandoned its long-held profit margin target in an effort to better defend its market position.[60] Strike three.

While some warning signs were present - including long-time owner Woodford bailing on Tesco in early 2012 (and laying out a solid rationale for his exit) - the combination of Tesco's distinguished dividend track record, its vast real estate holdings, and its leading share of the UK grocery market remained compelling reasons to hold and hope for a dividend turnaround.

Yet the numbers didn't lie. Tesco's dividend health slowly worsened and the dividend yield steadily increased to more than twice the U.K. market average (usually a good sign that something's wrong). It was only a matter of time before the board needed to make some tough decisions.

	Feb. 2014	Feb. 2013	Feb. 2012	Feb. 2011	Feb. 2010
Free cash flow coverage	0.59	0.18	0.59	0.66	1.78
Earnings coverage	1.61	1.17	2.51	2.57	2.41
Dividend per share	14.76p	14.76p	14.76p	14.46p	13.05p
Interest coverage	5.89	4.92	6.65	6.10	4.77

Source: Company filings, Morningstar.com

In August 2014, Tesco announced it would cut its interim dividend by 75%. A month later, it disclosed it had overstated its profit forecast for the year. In January 2015, Tesco canceled its dividend for the following fiscal year.[61,62] This was truly a brutal end to what initially appeared to be a high-quality dividend investment.

Lessons Learned: Tesco

• **Management changes matter:** When a very successful CEO retires or leaves a company for non-obvious reasons (e.g. he or she isn't 65 or older and looking to retire, etc.), it's time to reassess your investment thesis. In June 2010, well-regarded Tesco CEO Terry Leahy, who during his 14-year tenure more than quadrupled Tesco's sales and pre-tax profits, took many by surprise by announcing his retirement as of March 2011 at the still-young age of 55 while the company still had a number of unfinished projects overseas.[63,64] With the benefit of hindsight, this was an early red flag that changes were afoot and that all may not be well. Though a major management change in itself may not be a good reason to sell your position, an important change like this during a critical time should result in the company being closely monitored in coming quarters for signs of trouble.

• **Pay attention to dividend growth trends:** The fact that Tesco slammed the brakes on its dividend growth rate after years of solid increases was a sign that management and the board were growing concerned about the underlying business. Highly cyclical companies like materials, energy, and semiconductor companies may prudently hold their payouts flat for a year or two during a down cycle, but this generally shouldn't happen at companies in more defensive industries like food retailing, consumer goods, or utilities. When it does, something's up.

• **Free cash flow can tell a different story than earnings cover:** As the above table shows, Tesco's dividend looked well covered by earnings, but wasn't covered by free cash flow. Instead, Tesco supported its dividend through real estate monetization (i.e. sale and leaseback arrangements, etc.) and not by free cash flow generated through operations. Put simply, that's not a sustainable strategy. It took me too long to recognize the problem with my own investment in Tesco. Bottom line: if the company isn't covering its dividend with free cash flow, you at need to ask tough questions about how the company plans to afford its payout going forward.

• **Watch out for big capital investment misses:** When companies make large investments that ultimately fail, it can cause the board to reevaluate its dividend policy. Tesco's board may have, for instance, increased the dividend in prior years under the assumption that the investments in North America and China would work out. A big swing and miss may also require the board to reprioritize cash flows to pay down debt incurred to fund the investments.

Key Takeaways

- ➢ A good dividend track record in itself is a positive sign that the dividend is an important part of the company's capital allocation process, but there's no such thing as a bullet-proof dividend. If companies feel the pinch from creditors or see major problems down the road, what's happened with the dividend in years past matters little.
- ➢ Pay attention to the company's credit rating. If it has investment-grade credit ratings but just barely, the company may be more inclined to cut the dividend in bad times in order to maintain its investment-grade rating.
- ➢ Companies' dividend policies don't exist in isolation. Boards and management teams are always taking a look at their competitors' policies, too. If a company feels it's being placed at a competitive disadvantage by paying out more than its peers, a dividend cut could be on the horizon.

➢ Rapid dividend growth from cyclical or commodity-dependent companies is often too good to be true. As such, don't anchor your dividend portfolio in these companies and be more inclined to sell highly-cyclical companies after a good run than you would a more defensive or stable business.

Chapter 7: Where to Find Differentiated Dividend Ideas

Everything popular is wrong. – Oscar Wilde

In 2014, U.S.-based dividend-themed exchange traded funds brought in over $10 billion is new assets.[65] And this after $29 billion in 2013, when fully 13% of <u>all</u> U.S. ETF inflows went to dividend-based strategies.[66,67]

Many of the most popular dividend ETF strategies are focused on larger firms with good balance sheets and a long track record of increasing dividend payouts. These sort of high-quality, large-cap dividend payers are a relatively scarce asset. Indeed, in addition to creating a multi-billion-dollar business, it takes ten years of consecutive dividend growth to be added to most of these portfolios.

To illustrate, thousands of companies are listed on the U.S. market, but as of December 2015, only 51 companies are included in the S&P 500 Dividend Aristocrats (25+ years of consecutive dividend increases), 101 companies are held in the broader SPDR S&P Dividend ETF (25+ years of consecutive dividend increases), and 262 are held in the PowerShares Dividend Achievers ETF (10+ years of consecutive dividend increases).[68,69,70]

A scarce asset indeed.

Though companies with long dividend increasing track records make for fine investments, given the limited supply of such companies and the added interest in higher-yielding stocks during the zero-interest-rate era, finding values in this space has been understandably difficult. To get started, search for companies in the following areas, which typically don't show up in popular dividend lists and screens.

1. Firms that have cut their dividend

I realize this is borderline heresy in the income investing world. Though I've generally guided against investing in firms that have cut their dividend payout within the last five years, it's worth investigating each cut on a case-by-case basis.

Why did the company cut its payout? If it was one of the 1,000+ U.S.-listed companies that cut their dividend during the financial crisis, for example, there may have been a genuine concern for liquidity. This could have been due to an ill-timed acquisition or investment made in 2007 or 2008 that leveraged the balance sheet. In other words, the decision may not have been based on the board's long-term outlook, but on a legitimate short-term concern.

While most dividend cuts come *after* a sustained period of poor operating performance, some firms slash their payouts ahead of poor operating performance or if there's a need to retain cash for reinvestment needs. This happened at **WD-40**, maker of the eponymous household product, in 2001. At the time, the company was paying out nearly all of its net income in dividends and had done so for more than a decade.[71]

In March 2001, WD-40 decided a dividend cut was in the company's best long-term interest. As painful as the cut may have been for investors attracted to the company's high yield, the cut also enabled the company to pay down debt from recent acquisitions and grow in the longer-term. Patient shareholders have been rewarded as the stock returned nearly 650% return (dividend-adjusted) from March 2001 to December 2015.[72]

The key is to determine if management will capitalize on the dividend cut by changing the company's direction for the better – paying down debt, reinvesting in smart growth initiatives, etc. – or if they'll simply continue doing what they were doing before the cut.

Another post-dividend cut turnaround is **Dow Chemical**, which in February 2009 cut its dividend for the first time in its dividend's 97-year history, from $0.42 per share each quarter to $0.15 per share.[73] The main reason for the cut, management reasoned, was to preserve the company's investment-grade credit rating amid a terribly-timed (with hindsight, of course) and massive acquisition of rival Rohm & Haas, which was announced in July 2008, just as the financial crisis was warming up.[74,75]

Incredibly, from May 2008 to March 2009, Dow's stock price fell over 85% from $42.98 to a low of $5.89.[76] As the global economy recovered, Dow's balance sheet improved, and the Rohm & Haas integration proceeded successfully, Dow's board gained confidence in the company's ability to generate steady cash flows.[77] Fast-forward to December 1, 2015 and Dow's stock price is about $53 per share and its dividend has been fully-restored to pre-cut levels. Dow is currently in discussions to merge with longtime rival, **DuPont**.

Of course you want to avoid owning a stock prior to a dividend cut, but once the deed is done, there's no harm in having a look. Not all dividend cutters will rebound as well as WD-40 and Dow have (so far, at least), of course, and it's important to proceed with a "once bitten, twice shy" attitude, but sometimes a dividend cut can give a company a new lease on life. And because many dividend investors shun companies that have cut their payouts in the recent past, these situations can present good opportunities for the enterprising investor.

2. Firms that are in the final stages of a deleveraging process

A company that's currently paying down a large debt balance may not pass dividend screens that have low-debt requirements. If the company is generating large amounts of free cash flow, however, it likely has the capacity to pay down debt. Once the debt levels have returned to normal, the company then reallocate that free cash toward dividend growth.

When considering a dividend-paying stock with above-average debt, have a look through the company's recent filings, conference call transcripts, and presentations. You want to determine if it's aggressively reducing debt with free cash flow. If the company is struggling to pay down debt, I'd pass on the idea, but if it is making progress and is approaching its target leverage ratios, it may be primed for dividend growth in the near future.

International Paper, for example, made a large and leveraged acquisition of Weyerhauser's North American packaging business in March 2008, just before the financial crisis got into full swing. At the time, IP was also in the process of transforming its business away from traditional forest products where competition was fierce and the digital revolution forced a secular decline in publication paper demand. Instead, IP moved toward consumer and industrial packaging where competitive dynamics were more favorable. A year later, near the bottom of the financial crisis, IP cut its dividend payout by a massive 90% in order to maintain its investment grade credit rating and reduce its leverage.[78]

Two years later, IP fully restored its pre-cut payout, meaningfully reduced its leverage, and began to earn its cost of capital again.[79] As of this writing in late 2015, its dividend is nearly 80% above its pre-cut payout and the stock has been a ten-bagger from its March 2009 lows. An impressive recovery, indeed.

Figure 9: International Paper Quarterly Dividend History, 1970-2015

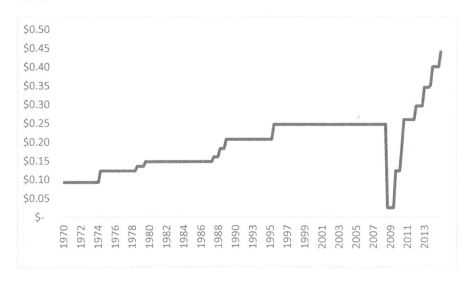

Source: Yahoo! Finance, author estimates.

3. Small caps

Traditional dividend analysis typically focuses on larger stocks due to their perceived safety (i.e. more financial resources and lower chance of going bust) and steers clear of small caps for the opposite reasons. On the contrary, there are plenty of smaller firms with good competitive positions, solid balance sheets, impressive management teams, and a distinguished dividend track record that I would consider just as steady as blue chip firms. Moreover, they may be more nimble in reacting to rapidly-changing markets compared with large caps, which tend to alter their course with the agility of an ocean liner.

A classic example of a quality small-cap is U.K.-based electrical equipment company, **FW Thorpe**, which has increased its payout each year since 2002 (including periodic special dividends) and has traditionally kept a clean, debt-free balance sheet. Further, as of this writing, descendants of the founder continue to own over 40% of the company, which I believe gives the company a relatively rare ability in the public markets to think longer-term and suffer through short-term hiccups.

The small cap universe is much broader than the well picked-over large cap space. Certain small caps may also have longer growth runways than their larger peers. As such, they shouldn't be overlooked.

When evaluating small cap dividend-paying stocks, I look for the following attributes:

1. **Low debt or preferably no debt.** Diversified, larger firms can get away with having more financial leverage and can typically get better rates on their borrowings, whereas smaller companies tend to be more cyclical or more reliant on one product line, so a rock-solid balance sheet is a must-have for a smaller company that pays a dividend.

2. **An invested leadership team.** With small caps, I like to see insiders own at least 5% of the company. Having some skin in the game should motivate management to allocate capital with a long-term ownership perspective in mind.

3. **Steady free cash flow generation.** This is always necessary when evaluating dividend-paying stocks as dividends must ultimately be funded by free cash flow in order to be sustainable. It's a particularly good sign when a small company is able to generate free cash flow across the business cycle.

4. **Dominant in a profitable market niche.** Small companies with dominant shares of niche markets may be less likely to attract the attention of large competitors. That's because the niche could be too small to make a difference for the large competitors. If the niche is attractive enough, the larger companies are

more likely to simply acquire the dominant player instead of entering the market themselves.

5.   **Operates in a decidedly boring industry.** I like to see a small company operating in an industry that's unlikely to attract investor attention – e.g. industrial parts, safety equipment, and food processing equipment. The longer the business can fly under investors' radars and not be of interest to potential competitors, the better.

6.   **A payout ratio below 50%.** Small companies with a long growth runway should be reinvesting at least half their cash back into the business to fuel long-term dividend growth. A firm that is paying out much more than 50% of its earnings is likely in the mature or declining stage of its lifecycle.

Researching smaller cap dividend-paying stocks requires a bit more legwork than researching large caps where information and analysis is more plentiful. If you're looking for firms with strong capital return potential, however, it can be a good place for dividend-minded individual investors to spend their researching time.

4. Spin-offs

Screens that require a long dividend history won't likely pick up on recent spin-offs, yet these can be great opportunities – not just on a dividend basis, but also on a value basis as they tend to have less initial analyst coverage and institutional interest.

Spin-offs also tend to be in good financial health. As Peter Lynch wrote in *One Up on Wall Street:*

> *"Large parent companies do not want to spin off divisions and then see those spinoffs get in trouble, because that would bring embarrassing*

publicity that would reflect back on the parents. Therefore, the spinoffs normally have strong balance sheets and are well prepared to succeed as independent entities."

Lists of upcoming and recent spin-offs are easily found online. Not all spin-offs make for good dividend holdings, of course, so I suggest focusing on the parent's dividend record and philosophy, the composition of the new board (i.e., Are they from the parent company?), and the new company's recent free cash flow history.

To illustrate, when **Philip Morris International** was spun-off of **Altria** in early 2008, it began trading with a dividend yield near 4% and has since more than doubled its payout.[80] With hindsight it's easy to see that PMI was an attractive idea. It didn't take a great leap in logic at the time of the spin-off, however, to conclude that it would likely follow its parent's philosophy about raising dividends (Altria has increased its dividend 49 times in the last 46 years).[81]

5. Low-yield companies with potential to rebase their dividends higher

Every so often a company that either doesn't pay a dividend or pays an insignificant one will rebase its payout much higher or initiate a sizeable dividend.

Case in point is **Apple**'s decision in March 2012 to initiate its first dividend payment since 1995. By early 2012, Apple was already the most valuable company in the world. It had revolutionized the mobile phone and computer industries with the iPhone and iPad, and became one of the best growth stock and turnaround stories of all time under Steve Jobs.[82]

Though Apple clearly still had growth ambitions, by early 2012 it was becoming clear that the law of large numbers would likely have an impact on the company's long-term growth rate.[83] As such, the high-growth investors that had courted Apple during its meteoric rise were perhaps a little less enthusiastic than they once were. By initiating a dividend, Apple's board likely saw an opportunity to appeal to a new category of investors – specifically, value- and dividend-minded investors - and lighten the company's growing cash pile.

On the date of the announcement, Apple's implied starting dividend yield was about 1.8%, in line with its large cap dividend-paying tech peers like **IBM**, **Cisco**, and **Oracle**.[84,85] In the three years following its first dividend payment, Apple has increased its payout by more than 37%.

Granted, these rebasing scenarios are rare and hard to predict before they happen. Once a company makes the decision to initiate or significantly increase its dividend, though, it's a pretty good sign that management and the board consider the dividend to be an important part of its capital allocation strategy going forward. Accordingly, it can be worth doing some research when you see a company adjusting its payout materially higher or initiating a considerable dividend.

6. Foreign Companies

As a group, investors have a well-documented "home-bias" toward companies based in their own countries, even though numerous studies have shown the benefits of global diversification.[86] Looking abroad for dividend ideas is particularly important if you live in a country where the stock market is heavily-weighted toward specific industries like commodities, banks, or energy and lacks exposure to other desirous sectors. The U.S. market, for example, has a very broad range of dividend-paying technology companies to consider like Apple and **Intel**, while the European markets are home to many of the world's largest consumer goods companies like **Nestlé** and **Diageo**. Some foreign markets also have investor bases that place a greater importance on dividends and conservative balance sheet health, which can be appealing in some situations.

Before adventuring overseas for dividends, however, investors should be aware that foreign companies can have different dividend practices. In some countries, for instance, it's common for companies to pay dividends once or twice per year while a quarterly dividend is more typical in the U.S. market. Second, investors should note any tax implications from receiving foreign dividends.

Finally, currency impacts can cut both ways – when your home currency is weak relative to the foreign currency in question, you receive a larger payout. The opposite is true when your home currency is strong relative to the foreign currency. Because of this factor, the value of your foreign dividends may fluctuate more on a year-to-year basis than those paid by domestic companies.

Key takeaways

> Most dividend investors are scouring established large caps with long track records of increasing dividend payouts. As such, it can pay to look for opportunities elsewhere, especially among small caps.
> Income investors often view companies that have reduced their dividends in the last five years as untouchable. If the company is deleveraging with ample amounts of free cash flow, however, it could present a compelling opportunity.
> Companies with rich dividend histories that have fallen on tough times due to cyclical headwinds, extreme circumstances (e.g. the financial crisis), or a poorly timed acquisition, may be more inclined to restore the dividend quickly once the company's returned to firmer ground.
> Spin-offs are typically under-covered by Wall Street and generally less known to investors, so an early bird can definitely get the worm. I'd be particularly interested if

the new company generates a lot of free cash flow and intends on paying a decent dividend as part of its capital allocation strategy.

➢ Former high-growth companies that are moving into mature growth stages face changing shareholder bases, as the growth investors rotate into more exciting prospects and value investors begin to get interested. Because of this, transitioning companies may be more inclined to initiate or rebase their low dividends closer to the market average.

Chapter 8: When to Sell a Dividend Stock

You have to inoculate yourself against regret. –
Daniel Kahneman[87]

The vast majority of the ink spilt in investing books is spent on how to make better buying decisions. Researching and buying a new stock can be fun and exciting. You've done the detective work, considered various outcomes, and decided this stock is the right place for new money. Your conclusions may be proven wrong, of course, but the initial feeling after hitting the buy button should be one of optimism.

On the flip side, the decision to sell a stock is more complicated and difficult. When you're selling a stock, you've either made money or lost money on the investment. Both scenarios present their own set of challenges.

If you're selling a stock that you've made a good deal of money on and it continues to pay attractive dividends, you may be reluctant to sell it. Loyalty is a wonderful trait to have in many aspects of life, just not in investing. Sure, as long as the company continues to perform well and isn't wildly overvalued, by all means hold onto it. Bear in mind, though, that a stock doesn't know how long you've owned it. It won't treat you any differently from someone who bought it this morning.

There's an entirely different set of emotions when you're faced with selling a stock for a loss. Behavioral research has shown that the average investor feels the pain of a loss two to two-and-a-half times more than when we enjoy similar sized gains.[88] As such, investors are often hesitant to sell when they're underwater on their investment. They hope to get back to "break even" before selling, simply because they don't have to realize the loss and regret the original buy decision.

The problem is that getting back to breakeven could take a long time to happen – if it ever does. Anchoring into your cost basis as a baseline for selling decisions can cause even more regret if the stock falls further. As we'll see in a moment, holding on in the face of a paper loss can be a fine strategy as long as you remain confident in the long-term outlook of the business, but you should always be ready to cut ties if the situation changes.

While there are some bad reasons for selling stocks, here are three situations where a sale is likely the most prudent action.

Your original thesis is broken

An obstacle to overcome when selling is "thesis drift." Thesis drift is when you make an investment for one set of reasons and then rationalize whatever happens next. Either you don't want to acknowledge things have changed or you simply forgot why you bought the stock in the first place. Before buying, then, it's helpful to write down five or more reasons why you'd want to own the stock. This way, if something changes about the underlying business, you can quickly refer to your original thesis and decide whether or not it is broken.

To illustrate, you might determine that a hypothetical dividend stock is attractive for the following set of reasons:

- The company dominates its competitors by having a library of valuable patents.
- The company generates high margins and returns on capital.

- Current management has a distinguished track record of conservatively and profitably growing the company and making smart bolt-on acquisitions.
- The current dividend policy is to maintain a coverage ratio of two times free cash flow; the payout looks safe and poised to grow.
- Insiders have invested large amounts of their personal wealth in the stock, which should better align their interests with common shareholders.

By writing down these reasons before making the investment, you can periodically review them to see if your original thesis still holds. If the company's patents are expiring soon or its margins are declining, it's time to revisit your valuation assumptions. After updating your outlook, your estimation of the company's value could now be below the market price and could warrant a sale. Alternatively, if the company holds its dividend flat or if dividend cover falls well below two times free cash flow, it's likely a sign that the competitive landscape and/or the company's strategy has changed for the worse.

More broadly, if you find yourself making a lot of excuses for a company's missteps, it's time to revisit your investment thesis. Remember, you don't work for the company's public relations department and there's no reason to spin bad results in a positive light. Call them as you see them.

When a thesis is broken, what remains is hope and emotion in the investment. That's a dangerous business.

Investors that hold close to traditional value investing rules generally make the argument that you should sell a stock when it reaches your fair value estimate. While this is a reasonable approach in some cases – particularly if you strategically bought an average or below-average company at a deep discount – it also has its flaws. If the company in question is well-run with durable competitive advantages, plenty of growth potential, and a good management team, you may be cutting yourself off from future gains by selling too soon. To paraphrase Peter Lynch, you don't want to cut your flowers to water your weeds.

Further, for income investors that aim to hold for the longer-term and place more emphasis on income generation, a fairly-valued stock with a still-intact thesis may be worth holding. If the stock shoots well past your fair value estimate – say, 30%-plus – then *that* is probably a good time to revisit your valuation assumptions. You may find that your original valuation assumptions were too conservative and you need to increase your fair value estimate. If nothing's changed, consider selling and rotating into a more attractively-priced investment.

Again, the key phrase here is *significantly* overvalued. While we may lace together an impressive valuation spreadsheet that tells us a stock is worth exactly $43.13 per share, we should also acknowledge the lure of false precision. It's nice to think we can pinpoint the valuation of an always-changing company in an always-changing marketplace, but the odds are low. Instead, use different scenarios to think about fair value "ranges."

To illustrate, if you're using a discounted cash flow or dividend discount model to value a stock, try creating a 5x5 table driven by your two major valuation factors to consider alternative scenarios.

Cost of Equity

		8%	8.5%	9%	9.5%	10%
	10%	$89	$82	$75	$70	$65
	9%	$83	$76	$70	$65	$61
Growth Rate	8%	$77	$70	$65	$60	$56
	7%	$70	$65	$60	$55	$52
	6%	$65	$59	$54	$50	$47

By thinking about valuation in terms of ranges rather than a specific amount, you give yourself some mental and emotional flexibility in case your analysis wasn't perfectly accurate (it rarely will be). You can also get a better feel for when the market might be pricing in unsustainable growth rate assumptions. For example, if the hypothetical stock analyzed in the table above is trading for $90, the market is more likely than not pricing in growth rates or a cost of equity that you don't think is reasonable. It may therefore be time to sell.

Alternatively, if you're valuing a company using relative multiples to its peers (price to earnings, price to book, etc.), consider both the stock's and its industry's historical multiples and what could be behind the current multiples. For example, let's stay you're researching a well-run consumer goods company with a forward price/earnings ratio of 22 times. Over the last 10 years, its forward price/earnings ratio has averaged between 14 and 18 times and the industry has averaged between 13 and 17 times. Assuming there's no major positive changes at the company or in the industry, this may be a good time to consider a sale since the current multiple is considerably above historical averages. I'd be less inclined to sell around 18 times, especially if I'm otherwise happy with the company's operations.

Be particularly careful using relative valuation selling rules with companies in cyclical industries (e.g. semiconductors, industrials, energy, etc.) as they tend to sell with cheap-looking price/earnings multiples near the peak of their cycle – when earnings are high – and expensive-looking multiples near the bottom – when earnings are low. Consider that in 2013, when WTI crude oil prices were around $100 a barrel, energy giant **Exxon Mobil**'s trailing price/earnings ratio ranged between nine and 13 times.

As I write this in early 2016, with WTI crude oil price near $30 a barrel, Exxon's trailing price/earnings ratio is around 20 times.[89] In some cases, cyclicals might even have negative price/earnings ratios during a downswing if they've failed to turn a profit. If anything, then, it could be a good time to sell cyclical companies when they look disproportionately cheap on relative valuation metrics.

However you approach valuation, the key is to have a send of what prices may be "fair" and which may be exaggerated and worthy of sale consideration.

You have a better place for the money

Investors need to consider reinvestment risk before selling a stock. Put another way, if you're swapping one stock for another, or into cash, there's a risk that the new investment won't perform as well over time. Still, there can be times when it makes sense to sell a lower-conviction current holding for a more compelling, high-conviction opportunity.

The level of your conviction can be determined by a blend of quality and value factors. For example, if the main reason you bought a stock was for its quality – you had high conviction that the company has considerable durable competitive advantages, plenty of growth potential, a rock-solid balance sheet, and a crack management team - it could turn into a lower-conviction name if those quality factors begin to deteriorate.

On the other hand, if you were agnostic about a company's quality, but you purchased it at what you considered a wonderful price, then the stock can become lower conviction as it approaches your fair value estimate, assuming no major changes in your quality analysis.

A helpful trick I learned from Richard Beddard of *Interactive Investor* was to draw up a 2x2 matrix with quality on one axis and value on the other.[90]

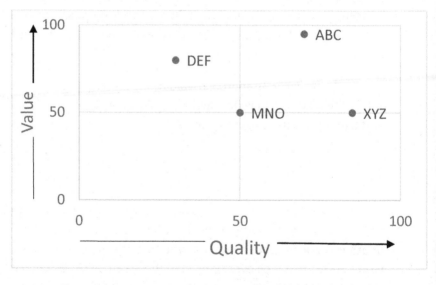

Here, I've plotted four hypothetical companies (represented by tickers ABC, DEF, MNO, and XYZ) with 100 being the best score and zero the worst, based on how I think they currently stand on the quality and value spectrum.

If I originally bought a share like XYZ that I think of as very high quality and consider it trading near fair value today, I'd be more inclined to hold it than I would a company like MNO which I see as having average quality and value. Similarly, if XYZ's quality were to deteriorate in my eyes, I'd be more prepared to sell as it moved left along the quality axis.

When to sell wonderful businesses

Here's a scenario I'm often asked about. You own a stock that pays a solid and steadily-growing dividend, has considerable pricing power, a sterling balance sheet, and is led by a skillful group of managers. Put simply, you consider it a wonderful business. When, if ever, should you consider selling such a company?

Theoretically, every stock in your portfolio should be available for sale every day for the right price. If someone wants to give you $1.25 in exchange for your $1 bill, well, that's a good deal, right? However, investors should be much more reluctant to part with wonderful businesses due to valuation alone since such a business's results can often far exceed your original assumptions.

By no means is my opinion here original. In his 1987 letter to Berkshire Hathaway shareholders, Warren Buffett wrote:

> *When we own portions of outstanding businesses with outstanding managements, our favorite holding period is forever. We are just the opposite of those who hurry to sell and book profits when companies perform well but who tenaciously hang on to businesses that disappoint.*[91]

Great, but why is this so? The most important answer lies in the math – specifically, the compounding potential of the underlying business. Here's Buffett's investing partner, Charlie Munger:

> Over the long term, it's hard for a stock to earn a much better return than the business which underlies it earns. If the business earns 6% on capital over 40 years and you hold it for that 40 years, you're not going to make much different than a 6% return—even if you originally buy it at a huge discount. Conversely, if a business earns 18% on capital over 20 or 30 years, even if you pay an expensive looking price, you'll end up with a fine result.[92]

In other words, if you have a wonderful business and paid up a bit for it (or hold it at elevated valuations), it may still be a much better investment than one you could have made in a mediocre business trading at a deep discount to its fair value. Defensible business models are rare, and especially so when they're managed by superior capital allocators who place a high priority on dividends. When you think you've got one of these, there's little reason to sell when valuations look a little frothy.

In his classic, *Common Stocks and Uncommon Profits*, Philip Fisher made a convincing case that you have a much higher success rate determining whether or not you have found a wonderful business than you do figuring out how the stock will perform in the next few months. As long as you believe you've found one of these exceptional businesses, Fisher argued, "both the odds and the risk/reward considerations favor holding."[93]

Traditional value investors are often uncomfortable buying or holding onto stocks with premium valuations. Their concerns are valid, of course, as a company bought or held at a premium valuation can produce wholly unsatisfactory returns if the company proves unworthy of the premium. Reversion to the mean is a powerful force.

On the other hand, many investors (including me) have demurred at the prospect of buying or holding onto a wonderful business trading for more than 20 times earnings on principle and have deeply regretted it. In investing, errors of omission can be far more expensive than errors of commission. Some businesses are, in fact, truly deserving of that premium multiple and it's our job as investors to figure out if the company is deserving of its premium multiple or not.

But how can we begin to tell the difference between a wonderful business worth holding indefinitely and just a decent one that should be sold when an attractive price presents itself? You want to be confident that the company has a durable competitive advantage and has a skilled management team with long-term investors' interests at heart. They broadly increase the dividend in-line with earnings growth, aren't reckless with the balance sheet, and only buyback stock when it's trading at a good-to-fair price.

A key caveat here is that you must remain vigilant in keeping up with the business to determine whether or not its "wonderfulness" might be dimming due to intensifying competition, internal mismanagement, or bad balance sheet decisions. If you think the company's quality is diminishing and permanently so, it may be undeserving of its premium multiple and may be a good sell candidate.

How to improve your selling process

We've already discussed reasons for selling, so we'll focus on three strategies we can employ today that can help us get better at selling stocks.

Do a "pre-mortem" before buying: One of my favorite questions to ask someone pitching a stock is, "If the stock price falls 30%, 40%, or 50%, what happened?" While a weak market may certainly play a role in any stock's decline, the point of the question is to determine what could go wrong at the company-level – new competition, a failed product, a bad M&A deal, etc. If you can determine what might go wrong *before* things actually do go wrong, you'll have a solid exit strategy to guide your future sell decision.

Review every sell decision, regardless of outcome: With every investment comes at least one valuable lesson that you can then apply to your decision-making process. As such, review each closed investment and determine what went along with your expectations, what didn't, and where you could have been more thorough in your research or decisions. Indeed, you may be quite content with your process and conclude that it was simply a poor outcome. Either way, it helps to make you a more thoughtful investor.

Create a "sold portfolio" and track its performance: Create a spreadsheet and track the performance of your sold stocks versus an appropriate benchmark (the S&P 500, FTSE 100, and so on). If you find that your sold stocks have *consistently* outperformed the market, it's time to reevaluate your selling strategy. Note that this effort will take some time to bear fruit as longer-term performance (at least three years) will be more telling than short-term results, which can be influenced by luck.

You'll notice that the common thread among these three strategies is to keep good records of your decisions. That's the key to improving any decision-making process as it reduces hindsight bias (i.e. "I knew this all along") and conservatism bias (i.e. being slow to incorporate new information or clinging to prior views).

Stop stop-losses

It's not an oversight that I didn't recommend stop-losses as a way to improve your selling process. They're probably great if you're trading stocks, but they aren't great if you're investing in stocks.

If you've done your homework, are comfortable with your thesis, and believe you paid a good-to-fair price for a competitively-advantaged and well-run company, why should it matter if the stock price temporarily falls 10%? If you approached the investment with a long-term mindset, what happens in the short-run matters very little, assuming there's no major change in the underlying business.

To paraphrase a line from Vanguard founder John C. Bogle, don't let the stock market be a distraction to the business of investing. Setting up stop losses may save you from some losses, but they can also prevent you from realizing some gains.

Admittedly, ignoring stock price fluctuations is easier said than done. So rather than executing a trade at a certain percentage price decline, try setting up an alert (via email, text message, etc.) if the stock price crosses that level. Then, take 24 hours to review your thesis and make a decision. Ready, aim, fire makes a lot more sense than ready, fire, aim.

Key Takeaways

- ➤ Knowing when to sell a stock can be emotionally more challenging than buying one.
- ➤ You should look to sell if your original investment thesis is broken, if the stock is significantly overvalued, or if you have a better place for the money.

➢ Wonderful businesses can be and should be held more patiently than businesses of fair quality.

➢ You can improve your selling process by doing a "pre-mortem" on all investments, reviewing past sell decisions, and maintaining a "sold portfolio" spreadsheet

Chapter 9: Keys to Dividend Reinvestment

"Shake and shake the catsup bottle. None will
come, and then a lot'll." – Richard Armour

Once you invest in a dividend-paying stock, it's essential to know what you're going to do with the income generated by your investment. This may sound like a minor point, but how you decide to reinvest can have a considerable impact on your long-term returns.

To illustrate, let's say you invested $1,000 in a stock 20 years ago that initially yielded 3% and subsequently grew in price by 8% per year. Using the "capital appreciation rate" (CAR) formula, we can see a considerable difference in your ultimate results, depending on what percentage of your dividends you reinvested in the stock over the period.

$$CAR = g + (1+g)*d*r$$

Where g = the annual price appreciation rate; d = initial dividend yield; r = % reinvested

Reinvestment Rate	CAR	Value After 10 Years	Value After 20 Years
0%	8.00%	$ 2,158.92	$ 4,660.96
25%	8.81%	$ 2,326.42	$ 5,412.23
50%	9.62%	$ 2,505.52	$ 6,277.63
75%	10.43%	$ 2,696.94	$ 7,273.47
100%	11.24%	$ 2,901.41	$ 8,418.21

If you took all of your dividends as cash and didn't reinvest (a 0% reinvestment rate), your capital value today was driven solely by price appreciation on your original investment. If, however, you fully reinvested all of your dividends over the

111

period (100% reinvestment), those little dividend payments also generated compounding returns, which substantially increased your capital value.

As we'll see, there's no "right" answer when it comes to reinvesting dividends, but it's important to understand this relationship of reinvesting and returns.

Your options

When you receive a dividend payment, you can do one of three things: you can save it, spend it, or reinvest it in the stock that paid it or in another stock.

The spending and saving options are fairly straightforward and are primarily used by investors who want to harvest the income from their portfolios to either support their lifestyles or to build up larger cash savings. There's nothing wrong with this strategy as long as the investor understands that not reinvesting can reduce their long-term capital appreciation rate.

Reinvesting, on the other hand, is primarily used by investors with a longer time horizon and those who don't need the income now. They're willing to sacrifice a little jam today for the potential of more jam tomorrow. There are two primary reinvestment strategies: the automatic and the manual method.

With *automatic* reinvestment, you instruct your broker to take any dividend received and buy more shares of the same stock that paid you the dividend. Under the *manual* strategy, you instruct your broker to put all of your dividends into your cash account and when you've saved up enough, you make a larger investment in your favorite idea at the time.

There are positives and negatives to both reinvestment strategies, but before you decide which one you'll use, here are six factors to consider.

1. Costs

Jack Bogle, the brilliant founder of Vanguard, is famous for his mantra: "Costs matter." The more you pay your broker when reinvesting, the lower your realized reinvestment rate. Over time, those costs and the lost compounding interest add up, so it's absolutely critical to keep trading costs as low as possible. For each trade you make – whether it's a large trade or a dividend reinvestment – a good rule is to keep costs below 1% (i.e. if you pay a $10 commission, invest at least $1,000 at a time). The lower, the better.

Check with your broker to see what type of fees might be associated with their dividend reinvestment scheme. Most US brokers don't charge for automatic reinvesting, but some brokers (particularly overseas, in my experience) may charge a fee for automatically reinvesting your dividends.

The size of your portfolio may help decide which option to use. For example, if you have a $20,000 portfolio with a starting yield of 4%, you would expect to generate about $800 in dividends in year one. If your broker charges a $10 trading commission then you'd be able to manually reinvest your dividends once per year and keep your trading costs around 1%. However, if your broker charges a 1% automatic reinvestment fee you might be better off with that option and keep your cash invested in the market (see key #2) versus sitting in cash earning very little, if any, interest for the better part of a year while you wait for your dividends to accumulate.

On the other hand, if you have a $100,000 portfolio with a starting yield of 4% and are generating $4,000 a year in dividends, you'd be able to make up to four fresh investments of $1,000 each year and keep costs around 1%. In this case, your dividends might only be sitting in cash for a few months and you can be more active with your manual dividend reinvestments.

It's important to note that if you have a small portfolio and are regularly adding fresh cash to it, you can consider lumping in dividend cash with fresh cash to make manual reinvestments. This would reduce the "waiting cost" for your cash not earning any interest.

2. Valuation

One of the benefits of manual reinvesting is that it gives you the opportunity to collect your cash and allocate it toward the most undervalued stock(s) in your portfolio. With automatic reinvestment, on the other hand, the cash is reinvested in the stock that paid the dividend without regard to timing.

In my mind, this does not necessarily make manual investing a clear winner. I'll expand on this notion in key #4 below, but sticking with valuation for a moment, as long as you are reinvesting in what you consider to be attractively-priced stocks, then either strategy can be beneficial.

If you're keeping a good watchlist that includes updated fair value estimates for your stocks, you'll have a better idea if and when your stocks become either under- or overvalued. If you're set up to automatically reinvest in an overvalued stock you can instruct your broker simply to not automatically reinvest that period. The dividend will instead go to cash and you can determine a better place for the money.

3. Be mindful of your broker's rules

Of course, the above strategy assumes your broker will allow you to choose a dividend reinvestment strategy on a stock-by stock-basis.

In addition, most brokers in the US will allow you to reinvest in less than one share, but some brokers may not. For example, if the stock trades for $50 per share and the dividend received is $25, some brokers will not allow you to buy 1/2 a share. Note that if you can't buy fractional shares, it reduces your reinvestment rate. If this will happen frequently in your portfolio, you may want to consider manual reinvestments and lump in dividends received with fresh cash added to the portfolio.

If your current broker's dividend reinvestment options are limited, see if another brokerage firm has more flexible reinvestment options. As long as the other broker's costs and services are similar, it might be time to switch brokers.

4. Know yourself

This point is critical: whichever strategy you decide upon, it's important to take into account your level of investing skill and discipline.

For instance, how good are you at determining a company's fair value? One of the benefits of automatic reinvesting is that while you'll probably buy more shares at elevated prices, you'll also likely pick up more shares at deep discounts. So if you're not keen on running discounted cash flow models or constantly comparing multiples, automatic reinvesting (all else equal) may be the better option. Automatic reinvestment is akin to dollar-cost-averaging – a strategy in which the investor invests a little money at a time on a regular basis into the same stock regardless of current market price.

If you choose manual reinvesting and don't have a good sense for valuation, you may end up allocating your cash to the wrong stocks at the wrong time. This can weigh on long-term returns. On the other hand, if you are in fact a highly skilled investor, you can greatly improve your long-term returns by allocating the incoming cash to the best opportunities.

Another question to ask yourself is: "How disciplined am I?" Manual reinvesting requires you to pay at least a moderate amount of attention to your portfolio and requires good record keeping (see #5); however, an investor who chooses automatic reinvesting could conceivably walk away from their portfolio for years (something I don't recommend) and will have had their dividends reinvested.

Be honest with yourself. If you don't have the time, discipline, or skill required for manual reinvesting it's probably best to stick with automatic reinvesting – again, assuming all else is equal (costs, broker rules, etc.). Keep it simple.

5. Keep good records.

Over time with automatic reinvestment, all of those little dividend payments and reinvestments add up and can become a bookkeeping nightmare. Each time you buy new shares through dividend reinvestment, for example, it adjusts your overall tax basis either upward or downward. In this sense, manual reinvesting can be much simpler since you aren't making as many tiny transactions. Bookkeeping, however, is not reason enough to choose one strategy or the other.

Whichever method you choose, it's essential to keep good and updated records – for both investing and tax matters. Keep and maintain a basic spreadsheet that tracks the income you receive from each stock as well as the prices paid for the stocks you bought via reinvestment.

Key Takeaways

- ➤ Which reinvestment strategy you choose can greatly impact your long-term capital appreciation rate.
- ➤ There's no perfect reinvesting strategy for all investors.
- ➤ The value of your portfolio and the amount of new cash you can regularly add to your portfolio will help determine the right reinvesting strategy for you.
- ➤ To maximize your reinvestment rate, aim to minimize commissions and taxes. Finding a broker with a good – and ideally, free – reinvestment option that allows you to buy fractional shares helps, as does keeping your dividend-paying stocks in a tax-advantaged account.
- ➤ Simple is better when it comes to reinvestment strategies. Whether you choose to automatically or manually reinvest, stick with the strategy with which you're most comfortable.

Epilogue

When we can never prove whether we really
know a thing, we must always be learning it. –
Seneca

Good dividend investing is simple: buy well-run businesses with decent yields and strong competitive positions at good-to-fair prices, then be watchful and patient. As simple as it sounds, it's not easy to implement.

The days of "buying and forgetting" dividend-paying stocks are over – if they ever really existed. In today's market, new and existing competitors alike are looking to disrupt high-margin, cash-flow generating businesses that are resting on their laurels. If a company's advantages are slipping, its profits and cash flows come under pressure and the dividend could therefore be at risk. Due to the ever-increasing competitiveness of the global markets, we can't remain ignorant of a company's competitive position and expect to do consistently well.

Further, companies are more willing – and often eager – to return shareholder cash via stock repurchases as an alternative to dividends. This is a major change from a generation ago when dividends were the primary means of returning shareholder cash. Buybacks, when properly used, can complement a good dividend quite nicely; however, many companies misuse buybacks and consequently destroy shareholder value. Because management's capital allocation decisions have a massive impact on both our capital and income returns, it's important that we learn to identify management teams whose interests are aligned with those of long-term shareholders.

Despite these new challenges, the core benefits of dividend investing remain strong. Someone buying his or her first dividend stock today has just as much of a chance at long-term success as someone who bought their first dividend stock 50 years ago. The major difference is that we must be more vigilant today. By avoiding the common mistakes made by dividend investors, considering a company's competitive advantages, forming an opinion on management, and recognizing the early signs of a possible dividend cut, we can greatly improve our chances of achieving satisfactory returns.

While there are a number fine investing strategies to consider, the key is to find and pursue the strategy that you find most intellectually and emotionally satisfying. If you don't find either of these things in a given strategy, you won't stick with the strategy long enough to see it through. Some investors prefer value investing, growth investing, mutual fund investing, and so on – and that's totally fine. Experience has taught me, however, that dividend investing has many traits that support an individual investor's inherent advantages – namely, our ability to be patient and think long-term.

I hope this book has helped you become a more thoughtful investor in general, and specifically a more thoughtful dividend investor. If you'd like to further your investment education, I've included a list of my recommended books and websites in the appendix. Thank you for reading.

Stay patient, stay focused.

Todd

Appendix 1: Glossary of Terms

Dividend: A cash payout made by a company to its shareholders.

Dividend per Share: The amount of cash paid to shareholders over the previous period (typically the past year), dividend by current shares outstanding.

Share Repurchase (Buyback): Cash used by a company to buy back its own shares in the market or via a tender offer to certain shareholders.

Earnings Coverage: Net income over a certain period (typically the past year) divided by dividends paid over the same period. The inverse of this equation is referred to as the "payout ratio."

Free Cash Flow (Equity): Cash available to common shareholders after a company has reinvested in its business. Free cash flow can be determined by subtracting capital expenditures (often referred to as "Purchases of Property, Plant & Equipment) from cash from operations. Both figures are found on a company's cash flow statement.

Free Cash Flow Coverage: Similar to earnings coverage, free cash flow coverage is determined by dividing a company's free cash flow over a certain period by dividends paid over the same period.

Economic Moat: A phrase coined by Warren Buffett to describe a company with durable competitive advantages, which enable the company to consistently generate returns on invested capital above its cost of capital. In other words, create shareholder value.

Appendix 2: A Dividend Checklist

One way we might improve our investing processes is to create checklists and review them before making buy and sell decisions. This is particularly true in stressful situations where our emotions can get the best of us. Rather than establish checklists with investment metrics (i.e. Does the stock have a price/earnings ratio below 15 times?), I find it much more helpful to ask myself behavioral questions. What I want to do is avoid making silly mistakes – ones I've made before and ones I've read about others making.

Here's a sample checklist I've developed for dividend investing. Feel free to use the ones you like, discard the ones you don't, and add your own as needed. No stock will receive a passing grade for every checklist question – if it does, your checklist is probably too lenient – but the key is to determine where your research may be deficient and where your risks may lie.

1. Can I explain to a six-year-old how the business makes money?
2. Am I buying this stock for its yield alone?
3. Am I buying this stock mainly because another investor I admire owns it?
4. Do I think I have a relatively good feel for this company's valuation?
5. Do I have a differentiated opinion about this company compared to the market consensus?
6. Am I basing this decision on what the company's done in the past rather than what it might do in the future?
7. Do I know what management's financial incentives are? Do I think they're appropriate?

8. Do I understand the competitive landscape(s) in which the company operates?
9. Would I feel comfortable locking in this investment for ten years and not being able to sell it during that time?
10. Will I enjoy owning and following this company?
11. Can I explain how this company will maintain its competitive advantages for more than ten years?
12. Will I be able to sleep at night?
13. Do I have an exit strategy if things don't go as planned?
14. Do I trust the CEO and CFO enough to leave my dog/cat/fish with him or her for the weekend?
15. Do I know the company's dividend policy?
16. Can I name the company's primary competitors? What do these competitors do better or worse than the company I'm researching?
17. How hard is it for a kid in his or her parents' basement to disrupt the company's business model sometime in the next five years?
18. Do I know the company's credit ratings?
19. Do I know if the company relies heavily on sales to one or two customers?
20. Do I understand the company's relationships with its stakeholders (shareholders, creditors, employees, suppliers, etc.)?
21. Does this company place a high priority on the dividend? How do I know this?
22. (For a current holding) If I woke up tomorrow and this stock had been sold overnight, would I buy it back right away?
23. Does this company have a unique corporate culture or business model?
24. Do I have a personal bias – positive or negative – toward the company's products?
25. Does the company prioritize dividends over buybacks?

Appendix 3: Financial Dividend Evaluation

The massive dividend cuts made by financial companies during the financial crisis years of 2008 and 2009 led a good number of dividend-minded investors to swear off all financial dividend payers. Understandably so. The financial crisis was a very challenging time for dividend investors. Many were burned by what they thought were well-run financial institutions.

Though we shouldn't forget the lessons from the financial crisis, I also think there's opportunity in the financial sector for dividend investors, precisely because so many have turned away from it.

That said, financial companies are a different animal from non-financials – their financial statements look different, "free cash flow" is more difficult to estimate since capital expenditures aren't clearly defined, etc. - so let's consider some factors that may point to a healthy dividend in the financial sector. (I've included a discussion of financial dividends and REITs in the appendix)

Management matters

First and foremost, management matters more in the financial industry than in any other sector. Because management teams at financial firms must make frequent and impactful decisions related to items like loan underwriting standards and balance-sheet strategy, it's absolutely critical to get a good understanding of management's strategy and capital allocation skill before investing in a financial firm.

Here are a few metrics you can use to gauge a management team's skill in the financial sector. They aren't meant to be a comprehensive blueprint for evaluating banks and insurers, but they're a start.

Banks

- **Efficiency ratio**: This measures how well a bank manages its overhead to generate revenues. The lower the metric, the better. Exceptional banks' efficiency ratios are consistently under 50%. This indicates that the bank incurred $0.50 in overhead costs to generate $1 in revenue. For some perspective, the average U.S. bank's efficiency ratio has been around 60%.[94]
- **Net interest margin**: Tells you the net interest (income minus expenses) realized from the bank's assets (loans and investments) and the cost of its liabilities (deposits). In general, the higher the NIM, the better. A NIM above 4% is a good starting point.
- **Return on equity**: Following the financial crisis, most regulators required banks to hold more equity capital on their balance sheets, which naturally lowered ROEs across the industry. A bank that's consistently generating ROEs above 10% in the post-financial crisis world with reasonable leverage is a positive sign.
- **Nonperforming assets/total assets (NPA Ratio)**: From the perspective of a long-term dividend investor, you don't want to own banks that consistently underwrite bad loans. As such, you want to keep an eye on a bank's credit quality trends over time. The NPA ratio is a good one to monitor. In good economic times, a bank's NPA ratio will usually drop below 1% as the bank's

124

customers are more likely to repay their loans on time. The inverse is true in recessionary environments and average NPA ratios will typically increase. An NPA ratio around 1% or below across the business cycle is generally an indication of a bank with decent underwriting standards.

Insurers

- **Combined ratio**: The combined ratio is the sum of the loss ratio, which measures how much the insurance company paid out in claims compared to the premiums it received, and the expense ratio (discussed below). The mix of loss and expense ratios will vary by company. Regardless of the mix, a combined ratio below 100% tells you that the insurance company's underwriting operations were profitable for the period. Insurers with combined ratios consistently above 100% need to rely heavily on strong investment returns to drive profit growth.
- **Expense ratio**: A component of the combined ratio, the expense ratio measures the efficiency of the insurer's underwriting business. Generally, the lower the ratio, the better, and a figure consistently below 20% usually indicates a very low-cost operation and possibly a durable competitive advantage.
- **Reserving practices**: Because the timing and amount of insurance claims are uncertain, all else equal, you want to look for insurers who consistently set aside more than they think they'll need to satisfy future claims. Conservative

reserving will depress current earnings, but is a sign that management is thinking longer term. If the claims that come in are lower than expected, the insurer also can "release" the reserves in future periods – a potential benefit for long-term shareholders.

More broadly, it's a good rule to be skeptical of any financial management team that says it's pursuing a high growth strategy. That's because durable competitive advantages are harder to find in the financial industry, with banks and insurers largely competing on price or interest rates. In other words, their products are, by and large, commodities. If the financial company in question is looking to hit the accelerator and take market share, it's likely doing so by cutting prices, making (potentially expensive) acquisitions, or offering higher interest rates to entice new customers. None of these are particularly encouraging signs unless you have high confidence in the management team.

Real estate investment trusts (REITs)

Over the last two decades, REITs have grown in popularity among income investors, primarily because they offer above-average dividend yields and are required by law (at least in the U.S.) to pay out at least 90% of their taxable income each year in the form of dividends.[95] In turn, the REIT pays very little if any tax on its earnings at the corporate level.

In general, there are two types of REITs in the U.S. – equity REITS, which typically own and lease income producing real estate such as office, residential, warehouse, and retail properties and mortgage REITs, which as their name suggests, own mortgages and make money off the spread between their borrowing and lending interest rates.

My focus here will be on equity REITs as I consider mortgage REITs much too risky for the average investor to have in his or her portfolio. Yes, mortgage REITs often feature enticing double-digit dividend yields, but that in itself should be a sign that the yields are too good to be true.

Equity REITs, on the other hand, can be very appropriate for individual investors who want some exposure to income-generating property markets but don't want to be someone's landlord. Each type of property comes with its own set of risks and opportunities – warehouses tend to do well when industrial demand is high, office properties could struggle if white-collar employment falls, shopping malls can do well if they can attract valuable tenants and have good foot traffic, and so on – but there are some general metrics and features to look for when evaluating a REIT.

- **Funds from operations (FFO)**: Net income isn't a great measure of a REIT's cash flow because the company needs to take large depreciation charges each year. Since depreciation is a non-cash charge, we add it back to the REIT's net income to arrive at FFO. From a dividend perspective, you usually want to see REITs consistently covering their payouts at least 1.2 times over with FFO.
- **Adjusted funds from operations (AFFO)**: This is the closest measure to "free cash flow" you'll find in the REIT world. The definition of AFFO may vary, but in its simplest form, it takes FFO and subtracts what the REIT needs to reinvest in its properties to maintain them (i.e. maintenance capital expenditures). You want to see REITs consistently cover their payouts at least once over with AFFO.
- **Fixed charge coverage ratio**: Similar to the interest coverage ratio we discussed earlier in the

chapter, the fixed charge coverage ratio (FFO / fixed expenses) measures the REIT's ability to pay fixed expenses (e.g. interest on debt, dividends to preferred stockholders, etc.) with regular cash flows from operations. A good rule of thumb is to look for a ratio consistently above 4 times.

Another thing to keep in mind when evaluating REITs is the type of leases offered to tenants. "Triple-net" leases that last for more than five years are on the more conservative and predictable side, since they require the tenant to pay for the property's insurance, taxes, and utilities. Shorter-term leases, like an apartment lease, can enable the REIT to quickly adjust to market conditions; however, they are also less predictable. With a short-term lease, a tenant can move out after a year at little or no cost if the new lease terms are unsatisfactory, or he or she decides to move.

Finally, because REITs regularly need to access the capital markets to fund their growth strategies, be careful of those that regularly dilute shareholders by issuing large amounts of equity – more than 5% annualized over longer stretches. Be particularly cautious of REITs that issue equity when their net asset values are above their market value, as they could mean they're selling their stock at bad prices. Unfortunately, this negative side effect of REITs isn't regularly discussed because most investors are focused on the high dividends being offered. Nevertheless, the dilution impact an important point to remember since your equity ownership stake in the company gets proportionately smaller (unless you buy more shares) as the company issues more stock.

Appendix 4: Reading Recommendations

This is the list of investing books and papers that I send people when they ask for reading recommendations. Presented in no particular order.

- Warren Buffett: Berkshire Hathaway Annual Letters
- Benjamin Graham. *The Intelligent Investor*
- Peter Lynch. *One Up on Wall Street*
- Guy Spier. *The Education of a Value Investor*
- Josh Peters. *The Ultimate Dividend Playbook*
- Don Schreiber, Jr. and Gary Stroik. *All About Dividend Investing*
- Ed Croft, Ben Hobson, and Dave Brickell. *How to Make Money in Dividend Stocks*
- Aswath Damodaran. *The Little Book of Valuation*
- Pat Dorsey. *The Five Rules for Successful Investing*
- Philip Fisher. *Common Stocks and Uncommon Profits*
- William Thorndike. *The Outsiders*
- Daniel Kahneman. *Thinking, Fast and Slow*
- Robert Hagstrom, *The Warren Buffett Way*
- Robert Hagstrom, *The Warren Buffett Portfolio*
- Robert Hagstrom, *Investing: The Last Liberal Art*
- Michael Mauboussin. *The Success Equation: Untangling Skill and Luck in Business, Sports and Investing*
- Michael Mauboussin. *More Than You Know: Finding Financial Wisdom in Unconventional Places*
- Stephen T. McClellan. *Full of Bull*
- Jim Slater. *The Zulu Principle*
- Joel Greenblatt. *The Little Book That Beats the Market*
- Aswath Damodaran. *Investment Fables: Exposing the Myths of "Can't Miss" Strategies*
- Burton Malkeil. *A Random Walk Down Wall Street*

- Robert F. Bruner. *Deals From Hell: M&A Lessons that Rise Above the Ashes*
- James J. Valentine, CFA. *Best Practices for Equity Research Analysts*
- Peter Bernstein. *Against the Gods: The Remarkable Story of Risk*
- Howard Marks. *The Most Important Thing*
- John Bogle. *The Little Book of Common Sense Investing*
- John Bogle. *Enough*
- Heather Brilliant and Elizabeth Collins. *Why Moats Matter*. (A little bias here -- I wrote Chapter 4 on equity stewardship)
- Tom Jacobs and John Del Vecchio. *What's Behind the Numbers?*
- Bruce Greenwald. *Competition Demystified*
- The Analyst's articles on dividend investing for the *Monevator* blog: www.monevator.com/tag/dividend-investing

Non-Investing Books With Lessons for Investors

- Robert Coover. *The Universal Baseball Association*
- Niccolo Macchiaveli. *The Prince*
- Laozi. *Tao Te Ching*
- Marcus Aurelius. *Meditations*
- Maria Konnikova. *Mastermind: How to Think Like Sherlock Holmes*
- Sir Arthur Conan Doyle. *The Adventures of Sherlock Holmes*
- Seneca. *Letters from a Stoic*
- Benjamin Franklin. *Autobiography*
- Malcolm Gladwell. *David and Goliath.*
- Ron Chernow: *Titan: The Life of John D. Rockefeller, Sr.*
- Robert Axelrod. *The Evolution of Cooperation*

Acknowledgements

To colleagues past and present, for your inspiration and education over the years.

An unexpected benefit of writing the *Clear Eyes Investing* blog and writing articles for a variety of publications is the connections I've made with people who've reached out to introduce themselves. Thank you to all the investors I've met electronically or in person over the years. I've learned a great deal from you.

Thanks to Mike, Owain, Gunnar, and Jeff for helping to greatly improve this book with your valuable edits and suggestions.

To my family, for your constant support and love.

To our loyal Labrador, Molly, for staying up late with me while I wrote.

To our son, Noah, for making me smile every day and helping me to appreciate the little moments in life.

To my wife, Kate, for your patience and encouragement and for traveling the world with me.

A.M.D.G.

About the Author

Todd Wenning, CFA is an equity analyst, investor, and writer based in Cincinnati, Ohio. You can contact him on Twitter @toddwenning or through his website, www.toddwenning.com.

Bibliography

[1] Barber, Brad M. and Odean, Terrance. "The Behavior of Individual Investors." September 2011. http://www.umass.edu/preferen/You%20Must%20Read%20This/Barber-Odean%202011.pdf

[2] JP Morgan Funds. "Guide to the Markets," U.S. Edition. November 2015. https://www.jpmorganfunds.com/blobcontent/759/582/1285893992869_MI-GTM_4Q15_Dec_highres-65.png

[3] Housel, Morgan. "Your Last Remaining Edge on Wall Street," *The Motley Fool*. June 2013. http://www.fool.com/investing/general/2013/06/18/your-last-remaining-edge-on-wall-street.aspx

[4] Tweedy, Browne Co. "The High Dividend Yield Return Advantage," 2014. http://tweedy.com/resources/library_docs/papers/HighDivStudyFUND2014Web.pdf

[5] Mackenzie, Michael and Oakley, David. "The Worst Year for Dividends Since 1938," *Financial Times*. March 2009. http://www.ft.com/intl/cms/s/0/4d750a32-075b-11de-9294-000077b07658.html

[6] Innosight. "Creative Destruction Whips Through Corporate America," 2012. http://www.innosight.com/innovation-resources/strategy-innovation/upload/creative-destruction-whips-through-corporate-america_final2015.pdf

[7] Macmillan, Douglas, and Telis Demos. "Uber Valued at More Than $50 Billion." WSJ. Accessed December 29, 2015. http://www.wsj.com/articles/uber-valued-at-more-than-50-billion-1438367457

[8] Lashinsky, Adam. "Amazon's Jeff Bezos: The Ultimate Disruptor." Fortune, 2012. http://fortune.com/2012/11/16/amazons-jeff-bezos-the-ultimate-disrupter/

[9] Gonzalez, David. "About New York; A Quiet Auditor Leaves Yeshiva a Fortune." New York Times. December 2, 1995. http://www.nytimes.com/1995/12/02/nyregion/about-new-york-a-quiet-auditor-leaves-yeshiva-a-fortune.html

[10] Yahoo! Finance. "3M: Historical Prices." Accessed January 2016. https://finance.yahoo.com/q/hp?s=MMM&a=0&b=2&c=1970&d=0&e =23&f=2016&g=d&z=66&y=0

[11] DQYDJ. "A Dividend Reinvestment Calculator for Any Stock." Accessed February 5, 2016. http://dqydj.net/dividend-reinvestment-calculator-for-any-stock-including-dollar-cost-averaging/

[12] Cowie, Ian. "10 Tips for Investing for Income from Neil Woodford and Others," 2010. http://blogs.telegraph.co.uk/finance/ianmcowie/100008092/10-tips-for-investing-for-income-from-neil-woodford-and-others/

[13] Tweedy, Browne Co. "The High Dividend Yield Return Advantage." http://www.tweedy.com/resources/library_docs/papers/TheHighDivA dvantageStudyFUNDweb.pdf

[14] Tweedy, Browne Co. "What Has Worked in Investing," 2009. http://tweedy.com/resources/library_docs/papers/WhatHasWorkedF undOct14Web.pdf

[15] Swedroe, Larry. "Swedroe: Dividends and Behavioral Econ." March 4, 2014. http://www.etf.com/sections/index-investor-corner/21413-swedroe-dividends-and-behavioral-econ.html?nopaging=1

[16] Dodd, David and Graham, Benjamin. *Security Analysis*. McGraw Hill. 1996. Page 320.

[17] "17 CFR 240.10b-18 – Purchases of Certain Equity Securities by the Issuer and Others." Cornell University Law School. www.law.cornell.edu/cfr/text/17/240.10b-18#

[18] Next plc. "Key Financial Information – Ten Year History." Accessed February 5, 2016. http://www.nextplc.co.uk/investors/key-financial-information/ten-year-history

[19] Next plc 2013 Annual Report and Accounts. http://www.nextplc.co.uk/~/media/Files/N/Next-PLC/pdfs/latest-news/2013/ar2013.pdf

[20] Thorndike, William. *The Outsiders: Eight Unconventional CEOs and Their Radically Rational Blueprint for Success*. Harvard Business Review Press. 2012.

[21] Offen, Scott; Rahman, Naveed; and Baumgardner, Emma. "Looking Backward and Forward at Dividend Growth." Published on Morningstar.com. April 1, 2014. http://news.morningstar.com/articlenet/SubmissionsArticle.aspx?sub missionid=188053.xml%20

[22] Morningstar.com, "Reynolds American: Price Ratios and Valuation," and "Wal-Mart: Price Ratios and Valuation," Accessed January 3, 2016. http://financials.morningstar.com/valuation/price-ratio.html?t=RAI

and http://financials.morningstar.com/valuation/price-ratio.html?t=WMT

[23] "WisdomTree Trust Domestic Dividend Funds Semi-Annual Report," September 30, 2008. Accessed via Morningstar.com. http://quote.morningstar.com/fund-filing/Semi-Annual-Report/2008/12/31/t.aspx?t=DHS&ft=N-CSRS&d=d87519cdb53fe9c6

[24] Mauboussin, Michael. "Anatomy of a Market Crash," Forbes.com. Published: October 2007. Accessed: January 3, 2016. http://www.forbes.com/2007/10/25/michael-mauboussin-crash-markets-marketsp07-cx_mm_1025mauboussin.html

[25] Damodaran, Aswath. "Ratings, Interest Coverage Ratios and Default Spread." Data as of January 2016. http://pages.stern.nyu.edu/~adamodar/New_Home_Page/datafile/ratings.htm

[26] Fisher, Philip. *Common Stocks and Uncommon Profits*. New York, Wiley. 2003.

[27] Reeves, Martin; Levin, Simon; and Ueda, Daichi. "The Biology of Corporate Survival," Harvard Business Review. January 2016. https://hbr.org/2016/01/the-biology-of-corporate-survival

[28] Ibid

[29] Berkshire Hathaway Annual Letter to Shareholders, 1987. http://www.berkshirehathaway.com/letters/1987.html

[30] Levy, Steven. "Jeff Bezos Owns the Web in More Ways Than You Think," Wired Magazine. November 13, 2011. www.wired.com/2011/11/ff_bezos/all/1

[31] The Coca Cola Company. "Investor Info: Dividends," Accessed December 1, 2015. http://www.coca-colacompany.com/investors/stock-history/investors-info-dividends/

[32] U.S. Department of Commerce. "How Long Does Patent, Trademark, or Copyright Protection Last?" http://www.stopfakes.gov/faqs/how-long-does-patent-trademark-or-copyright-protection-last

[33] Medtronic. "Medtronic Increases Cash Dividend by 25 Percent," June 19, 2015. http://newsroom.medtronic.com/phoenix.zhtml?c=251324&p=irol-newsArticle&ID=2060949

[34] Hom, Brian. "30+ Years in Operation Finalist: Jack Henry & Associates Inc." Springfield Business Journal. July 22, 2013. http://sbj.net/Content/Archives/Archives/Article/30-Years-in-Operation-Finalist-Jack-Henry-Associates-Inc-/48/108/94228

[35] "Jack Henry: Historical Prices." Yahoo! Finance.
http://finance.yahoo.com/q/hp?s=JKHY&a=02&b=26&c=1990&d=10&
e=16&f=2015&g=v

[36] Seeking Alpha. "Ecolab's CEO Hosts 2013 Investor Day (Transcript)."
Published September 12, 2013.
http://seekingalpha.com/article/1691682-ecolabs-ceo-hosts-2013-
investor-day-conference-transcript?part=single

[37] Ecolab. "Ecolab Increases Cash Dividend 6%." December 3, 2015.
http://investor.ecolab.com/news-and-events/press-releases/2015/12-
03-2015-185505522

[38] Taube, Aaron. "Why Costco Pays Its Retail Employees $20 an Hour."
Business Insider, October 23, 2014.
http://www.businessinsider.com/costco-pays-retail-employees-20-an-
hour-2014-10

[39] Byrnes, Brendan. "Costco Co-Founder: 'Culture Is Not the Most
Important Thing – It's the Only Thing." August 21, 2013.
http://www.fool.com/investing/general/2013/08/21/costco-leader-
culture-is-not-the-most-important-th.aspx

[40] Berkshire Hathaway Annual Letter to Shareholders, 2005.
http://www.berkshirehathaway.com/letters/2005ltr.pdf

[41] Ewing, Jack. "DHL to Halt Express Deliveries in the U.S." Bloomberg
Business. November 10, 2008.
http://www.bloomberg.com/bw/stories/2008-11-10/dhl-to-halt-
express-deliveries-in-the-u-dot-s-dot-businessweek-business-news-
stock-market-and-financial-advice

[42] *Outstanding Investor Digest*, June 30, 1993

[43] Mauboussin, Michael. *The Success Equation: Untangling Skill and
Luck in Business, Sports, and Investing.* Harvard Business Review Press,
2012.

[44] Berkshire Hathaway Annual Letter to Shareholders, 1987.
http://www.berkshirehathaway.com/letters/1987.html

[45] Arnott, Robert D. and Asness, Clifford S. "Surprise! Higher Dividends
= Higher Earnings Growth." *Financial Analysts Journal.*
January/February 2003.
https://www.researchaffiliates.com/Production%20content%20library
/FAJ_Jan_Feb_2003_Surprise_Higher_Dividends_Higher_Earnings_Gro
wth.pdf

[46] Siburn, Jonathan. "Admiral Founder Continues to Steer a Steady
Course." *The Telegraph.* March 7, 2010.
http://www.telegraph.co.uk/finance/newsbysector/banksandfinance/i

nsurance/7393039/Admiral-founder-continues-to-steer-a-steady-course.html

[47] Eldorado Gold. "Dividends," Accessed January 4, 2006. http://www.eldoradogold.com/investors/shareholder-information/dividends/default.aspx

[48] Van Cleaf, Mark; Leeflang, Karel; O'Byrne, Stephen. "The Alignment Gap Between Creating Value, Performance Measurement, and Long-Term Incentive Design." IRRC Institute. 2014. http://irrcinstitute.org/pdf/alignment-gap-study.pdf

[49] Silverblatt, Howard. S&P Dow Jones Indices. As of December 2015. http://www.spdji.com

[50] Wernau, Julie. "Exelon Cuts Dividend by 41%," Chicago Tribune, February 7, 2013. http://articles.chicagotribune.com/2013-02-07/business/chi-exelon-nearly-halves-its-dividend-20130207_1_exelon-shares-electricity-prices-exelon-ceo-christopher-crane

[51] Exelon. "Exelon Announces Fourth Quarter ad Full Year 2012 Results." February 7, 2013. http://www.exeloncorp.com/newsroom/Pages/pr_20130207_EXC_Q4 Earnings.aspx

[52] Pfizer, 2008 Annual Report. https://www.pfizer.com/files/annualreport/2008/financial/financial2008.pdf

[53] Sorkin, Andrew Ross. "Pfizer Agrees to Pay $68 Billion for Rival Drug Maker Wyeth," New York Times, January 25, 2009. http://www.nytimes.com/2009/01/26/business/26drug.html?_r=0

[54] Pfizer, "Pfizer to Acquire Wyeth, Creating the World's Premier Biopharmaceutical Company." January 26, 2009. http://press.pfizer.com/press-release/pfizer-acquire-wyeth-creating-worlds-premier-biopharmaceutical-company

[55] Pfizer, 2005 Annual Reporthttp://www.pfizer.com/files/annualreport/2005/annual/review2005.pdf

[56] Pfizer, 2007 Annual Report. https://www.pfizer.com/files/annualreport/2007/financial/financial2007.pdf

[57] Berkshire Hathaway Annual Letter to Shareholders, 1989. http://www.berkshirehathaway.com/letters/1989.html

[58] Tesco plc. 2011 Annual Report.
http://www.tescoplc.com/files/pdf/reports/tesco_annual_report_2011.pdf

[59] Sonne, Paul and Evans, Peter. "The $1.6 Billion Grocery Flop: Tesco Poised to Quit U.S." WSJ. December 6, 2012.
http://www.wsj.com/articles/SB1000142412788732464010457816051419269 5162

[60] Wood, Zoe. "Tesco Abandons Space Race and Invests Resources in New Price War." *The Guardian*. February 25, 2014.
http://www.theguardian.com/business/2014/feb/25/tesco-supermarket-price-cuts-profit-forecast

[61] Reed, Stanley. "Tesco Says It Overstated Profit Forecast." NY Times. September 22, 2014.
http://www.nytimes.com/2014/09/23/business/international/tesco-shares-slide-on-news-that-it-overstated-profit-guidance.html

[62] Tesco plc. "Trading Statement for 19 Weeks Ended 3 January 2015." January 8, 2015.
http://www.tescoplc.com/index.asp?pageid=188&newsid=1127

[63] Sibun, Jonathan and Fletcher, Richard. "Surprise as Sir Terry Leahy Resigns from Tesco." The Telegraph. June 8, 2010.
http://www.telegraph.co.uk/finance/newsbysector/retailandconsumer/7812463/Surprise-as-Sir-Terry-Leahy-resigns-from-Tesco.html

[64] Tesco, Annual Review,
2011.https://www.tescoplc.com/files/pdf/reports/tesco_annual_review_2011.pdf

[65] Shriber, Todd. "A Dandy Year for This Dividend ETF." ETF Trends. December 23, 2014. http://www.etftrends.com/2014/12/a-dandy-year-for-this-dividend-etf/

[66] Lydon, Tom. "No Surprise Here: Record ETF Inflows in 2013." ETF Trends via Yahoo! Finance. January 6, 2014.
http://finance.yahoo.com/news/no-surprise-record-etf-inflows-165519609.html

[67] Invesco PowerShares Capital Management LLC. "Invesco PowerShares Institutional Snapshot: Q1 2014."
http://www.invescopowershares.com/pdf/P-SNAP-FLY-1.pdf

[68] "S&P 500 Dividend Aristocrats." S&P Dow Jones Indices. Accessed December 2015. http://us.spindices.com/indices/strategy/sp-500-dividend-aristocrats

[69] "SPDR® S&P® Dividend ETF." State Street Global Advisors. Accessed December 2015.
https://www.spdrs.com/product/fund.seam?ticker=SDY

[70] "PowerShares Dividend Achievers Portfolio." Invesco PowerShares, as of September 30, 2015.
https://www.invesco.com/static/us/investors/contentdetail?contentl
d=b5d2fd05f0e21410VgnVCM100000c2f1bf0aRCRD&dnsName=us
[71] Palmer, Jay. "The Cult of WD-40." *Barron's*. December 3, 2001.
http://www.barrons.com/articles/SB1007175539633662160
[72] "WD-40: Historical Prices." Yahoo! Finance. Accessed: January 10, 2016.
http://finance.yahoo.com/q/hp?s=WDFC&a=02&b=27&c=2001&d=11
&e=1&f=2015&g=d&z=66&y=3630
[73] Hinton, Christopher. "Dow Chemical Lowers Dividend For the First Time." MarketWatch. February 12, 2009.
http://www.marketwatch.com/story/dow-chemical-cuts-dividend-first-time
[74] Moore, Heidi N. "Could Warren Buffett Save Dow Chemical?" WSJ. January 8, 2009. http://blogs.wsj.com/deals/2009/01/08/could-warren-buffett-save-dow-chemical/
[75] Campoy, Ana. "Dow Chemical Closes Rohm & Haas Deal." WSJ. April 2, 2009. http://www.wsj.com/articles/SB123860746676278981
[76] Yahoo! Finance: "Dow Chemical: Historical Prices: April 1, 2008 – June 28, 2009."
http://finance.yahoo.com/q/hp?s=DOW&a=03&b=1&c=2008&d=05&e
=28&f=2009&g=d&z=66&y=264
[77] Kaskey, Jack. "Dow Chemical Raises Dividend 67% Two Years After First Cut." Bloomberg Business. April 14, 2011.
http://www.bloomberg.com/news/articles/2011-04-14/dow-boosts-dividend-to-25-cents-a-share-from-15-cents-a-share
[78] International Paper. "International Paper Announced Reduction in Quarterly Dividend." March 2, 2009.
http://investor.internationalpaper.com/news-releases/Press-R/2009/International-Paper-Announces-Reduction-in-Quarterly-Dividend-ag2/default.aspx
[79] International Paper, "Investor Roadshow (Presentation): 4Q 2015."
http://s1.q4cdn.com/620066352/files/doc_downloads/Roadshow/201
5/November/Roadshow-Handout-11032015-WEBSITE.pdf
[80] Philip Morris International, "Dividend Schedule and History." Accessed December 2015.
http://investors.pmi.com/phoenix.zhtml?c=146476&p=irol-dividends
[81] Altria, "Altria Increases Quarterly Dividend by 8.7% to $0.565 per Common Share." August 21, 2015.

http://investor.altria.com/phoenix.zhtml?c=80855&p=irol-newsArticle&ID=2081218

[82] Satariano, Adam. "Apple Overtakes Exxon Becoming World's Most Valuable Company." Bloomberg Business. August 10, 2011. http://www.bloomberg.com/news/articles/2011-08-09/apple-rises-from-near-bankruptcy-to-become-most-valuable-company

[83] Stewart, James B. "Confronting a Law of Limits." NYT. February 24, 2012. http://www.nytimes.com/2012/02/25/business/apple-confronts-the-law-of-large-numbers-common-sense.html?_r=0

[84] Apple, "Apple Announced Plans to Initiate Dividend and Share Repurchase Program." March 19, 2012. https://www.apple.com/pr/library/2012/03/19Apple-Announces-Plans-to-Initiate-Dividend-and-Share-Repurchase-Program.html

[85] Goldman, David. "Apple Announces Dividend and Stock Buyback." CNN Money. March 19, 2012. http://money.cnn.com/2012/03/19/technology/apple-dividend/

[86] Philips, B. Christopher; Kinnery, Jr., Francis M.; Donaldson, Scott J. "The Role of Home Bias in Global Asset Allocation Decisions." Vanguard, June 2012. https://pressroom.vanguard.com/content/nonindexed/6.26.2012_The_Role_of_Home_Bias.pdf

[87] Housel, Morgan. "Daniel Kahneman: Don't Fall Victim to Regret." The Motley Fool. July 8, 2013. http://www.fool.com/investing/general/2013/07/08/dont-fall-victim-to-regret.aspx

[88] Mauboussin, Michael. *More Than You Know: Finding Financial Wisdom in Unconventional Places*. Columbia University Press. 2007.

[89] YCharts. "Exxon Mobil P/E Ratio (TTM)." Accessed February 6, 2016. https://ycharts.com/companies/XOM/pe_ratio

[90] Beddard, Richard. "Share Sleuth's Notepad: Matrix Reloaded." Interactive Investor. February 7, 2013. http://www.iii.co.uk/news-opinion/richard-beddard/share-sleuths-notepad-matrix-reloaded-0

[91] Berkshire Hathaway Annual Letter to Shareholders, 1988. http://www.berkshirehathaway.com/letters/1988.html

[92] Chew, John. "Wesco Financial's Charlie Munger." CS Investing (blog). http://csinvesting.org/wp-content/uploads/2014/05/Worldly-Wisdom-by-Munger.pdf

[93] Fisher, Philip. *Common Stocks and Uncommon Profits*. New York, Wiley. 2003.

[94] BankRegData. "Efficiency Ratio." Accessed January 8, 2016. http://www.bankregdata.com/allIEmet.asp?met=EFF

[95] "What is a REIT?" NAREIT. Accessed December 1, 2015.
https://www.reit.com/investing/reit-basics/what-reit

Made in the USA
Monee, IL
15 June 2022

98036405R00083